Blind Faith

Hebrews 11:1

MARK DOWDY

WITH

MICHELLE DOWDY

Mark

&

Michelle Dowdy

ISBN 978-1-0980-4573-9 (paperback)
ISBN 978-1-0980-4574-6 (digital)

Christian Faith Publishing, Inc.
832 Park Avenue
Meadville, PA 16335
www.christianfaithpublishing.com

Printed in the United States of America

Foreword

Almost a decade ago, I was honored to research and write the true story of one of our country's greatest heroes—a Navy SEAL named Adam Brown. The book is called *Fearless*, and some described the story as the prodigal son meets SEAL Team Six. In a nutshell, that fits. Adam was raised by a loving family, but after high school, he became addicted to drugs, faced multiple felony counts, and ended up in jail more than once. Through a miraculous series of events, he rose up from that dark time and turned his life around. He rose up to the coveted Navy SEAL Teams, but his challenges didn't stop there. He was plagued by injuries that warranted medical discharge, but he refused to retire. Even after losing his dominant right eye and the fingers on his dominant right hand, he silenced the naysayers, taught himself to shoot left-handed, and rose higher still to Navy sniper, and then to the top tier of US Special Operations Forces—SEAL Team Six. All the while, he was a loving husband, father, and son who credited his wife, Kelley, his family, his faith, and his friends for giving him strength.

Adam was killed in combat while protecting his teammates in Afghanistan. One of his final requests was that his whole story be told, including the dark times—times that even his children didn't know about. It was his last selfless and fearless act so that others might be inspired, to know that no matter how far you might fall, you can always get up and rise above your darkest hours.

Inspire, he did. Letters by the thousands came in, including one by a man named Mark Dowdy, who said, "I was so inspired by Adam's story, and I would love to honor the family and Adam in song with what I do—I'm a musician, I'm a singer, I'm a songwriter." I called Mark, and he told me there was another connection he had to Adam and left it at that. I didn't push. I felt it was private, that

3

perhaps Mark had been an addict or was struggling with something in his life.

Ultimately, Mark told me: he and Adam both shared a similar issue with vision. They both had undergone multiple corneal transplants, all of which failed in quests to regain their eyesight. I learned Mark, however, had been born blind in both eyes, and he told me that music had been his saving grace. Still I admit I held my breath when I first played the song he sent me. I was immediately blown away by his talent as a songwriter, singer, and musician. He captured Adam's story perfectly, and we immediately moved to make the song "Fearless" a part of events and media associated with the book.

As our friendship grew, Mark started telling me stories of the things he did growing up beyond playing the piano, guitar, and most any instrument he picked up. He did things blind—like riding a bicycle, which is tough enough when you've got two good eyes. He became an Eagle Scout and even passed the marksmanship badge qualifications by aiming at a bell that was rung in the center of the target. And there were funny bits like the time he admittedly drove a car, to the chagrin of the officer who pulled him over and told his copilot that it wasn't such a good idea even on country roads to direct a blind man But what really got me were the stories of all the painful surgeries in which he tried to regain his sight—especially the one when he had hope he might finally get to gaze upon his children and wife, whom he'd never seen but through the dark, shadowy haze of his blindness.

I won't tell you how that one turned out. I'll just say that of all the people I've met and written about, Mark Dowdy stands tall beside the men and women you might generally consider heroes. He stands as an example of what it means to have faith—*blind faith*, which is what I told him his book should be called when he decided to write it. "And by the way," I told him, "you can use that free of charge—just let me write the foreword."

Eric Blehm
New York Times bestselling author of *Fearless* and other titles
www.ericblehm.com
https://m.youtube.com/watch?v=HWG1O6SB-KM

Special Thanks

As I began writing this book, I thought about all the people who have had a part in what this story has become. There would be so many names to list, and I'm sure I would probably leave someone out. Of all the people who have influenced me the most throughout my life, one person stands out. A friend to many, to his grandchildren, he is Pops; to me, he is Dad—Bob Dowdy. He has championed so many causes on my behalf; he has been a constant source of great advice and has always been the best example of who a father should be. It is to him I dedicate this book. I love you, Dad!

Introduction

I was thirty-eight years old, and I had never seen my wife and children in detail. Having spent most of my life visually with only light/dark and color perception, I was about to undergo a procedure that would have the potential to change my life dramatically. It was a bright, crisp September day in 2003 when we went to the Emory Eye Clinic in Atlanta, Georgia, for the surgery to replace my clouded cornea with a young healthy one. My wife was with me in the pre-op area. I was nervous but at peace at the same time with my decision to try the surgery that could possibly take what little vision I had or open up a whole new world for me. For the surgery itself, I was in the very capable hands of Dr. Diane Song, who was probably younger than I was and had small delicate hands, perfect for her life's work. The anesthesiologist's name was Dr. Sung, and the significance of the names of these doctors was lost on no one.

Practically speaking, it was cold in the pre-op area, and being filled up with a bag of IV fluid, I kept wishing the surgical team would hurry it up because I had the urge to go to the bathroom every few minutes. Finally, it was time to go back to the operating room, and I was ready. This procedure, a corneal transplant, was outpatient surgery; and in fact, I was awake but sedated during the entire process. My eye was numb, but I was aware that my eye was being operated on, and I could see the surgical instruments as they came close to stitch the new cornea in place.

Out in the waiting room were my anxious family and friends, pacing and praying that this would be a procedure with miraculous results. I was sure that running through my parents' minds must have been all the previous failed surgeries, all the heartache they'd been through as young parents, and maybe their thoughts even went back to another hospital, when they first found out the painful truth that their son could not, and maybe would never, be able to see them or the beautiful world around him clearly.

Chapter 1

FIRM FOUNDATIONS

I was born August 28, 1965, in the Hall County Hospital to Bob and Wanda Dowdy, a young vibrant couple who already had one toddler, my sister Andrea, who was two years old at the time. My mother barely made it to the hospital before I was born and recalled the doctor telling her that if she had a third child, he would put her in the hospital around her due date to assure that she wouldn't give birth in the car. My mother's pregnancy was an easy one, with no morning sickness. I was born on a Saturday night, and both mother and father were pleased that they had a son to complete their family. But joy quickly turned to concern as my mother noticed that my eyes had an opaque look about them.

She recalls holding me for the first time and commenting to the nurses, "Something's wrong with this baby's eyes."

"No, no," they said, "he's fine."

But doctors would later confirm what she felt was true from the first time she held me. Two days later, Dr. John Burns, who had delivered me, came into my mother's room to deliver the news. A good friend of the family, Dr. Burns was heartbroken to confirm my mother's fears.

"You were right. He can't see," he said, his voice choking with emotion.

Seeking to be proactive, Dr. Burns had already contacted Dr. John Reed, a respected ophthalmologist in Gainesville, and he was to be there later in the day to talk with my parents about my condition. The real cause of my blindness was not known, as is the case with many birth defects. Doctors would later speculate that my mother might have been exposed to the measles virus while she was pregnant with me, even though she showed no symptoms of the disease itself. There had been an outbreak of measles on a local college campus during the time of my mother's pregnancy.

When I was five days old, an appointment was made for Dr. Reed to examine me in his office. He made a referral to another doctor at Emory University Hospital, and I was there for an office visit when I was two weeks old. Almost immediately, options were discussed for prospects of surgery to improve my vision, and my parents were willing to do whatever it took to improve my chances for a "normal" life. So began my journey, filled with doctor's appointments, transplant waiting lists, painful surgeries, and lengthy recoveries.

My parents brought me home from the hospital and soon adjusted to life with another baby in the house. They recall that I did seem to have a heightened sense of hearing even as a newborn. They soon learned that I would wake up anytime someone entered the nursery, even though they attempted to be as quiet as possible, and the floor was carpeted. I would also wake at the sound of a light switch being turned on or off. Even during this time, music was being introduced into my world; they placed a radio in the nursery, thinking this would mask the noises that would wake me. It didn't prove to be effective for that purpose but may have been part of what helped me develop a love for music early on. From the beginning, my parents tried not to set limits on me or my mobility and say they don't remember having to make any special adjustments in the house for my safety beyond what one would do for a typical baby. They let me explore the house, and I learned by trial and error where things were, first crawling and then walking, a little late, at about sixteen months old, which is typical for children with visual impairments.

During this period of time, I'm told my favorite "toy" was a record player. My parents would sit me in the floor and said I would listen for hours to whatever they played for me. I do have a vague recollection of this. I also had a toy piano that I would play while sitting on the floor. My mother remembers that I wouldn't just "bang" on the piano like a typical toddler but would hit the notes individually and tilt my head toward the sound.

Even as my parents watched me grow and develop that year, plans were underway for my first corneal transplant. I actually had my first surgery at Duke University Medical Center in Durham, North Carolina, in 1966 at age six months to remove a cyst from my left eye. My first cornea transplant was attempted at age thirteen months at Egleston Children's Hospital in Atlanta, Georgia. The procedure failed, my body rejecting the new cornea, which clouded over even before I'd left the hospital. Another transplant was performed in 1967 at age two years, also at Egleston. Despite the antirejection drug regimen and cutting-edge medical treatment of the day, that transplant failed as well. It would be the last surgery until 1972, at age six.

My earliest vivid memories began when I was three years old, and we moved into a new house. This home had two sets of steps and a basement with plenty of space to play. I remember receiving an electric car for Christmas that year and being able to ride it around and around in the big open space of the basement. My love for music was growing too, and by age six, I was being introduced to the popular songs of the day. My parents had bought an electric keyboard for me for Christmas when I was five years old. I would listen to the songs on my record player and then start to play along with the keyboard parts. The first song I ever played like that was "Have You Ever Seen the Rain?" by Creedence Clearwater Revival. I would start to sing along too as I was playing. I wasn't taking any keyboard lessons at that point, just picking out the notes by ear.

In those times, most blind children were sent to the Georgia Academy for the Blind in Macon, Georgia, to live on campus and learn the skills they would need to be as independent as possible. My parents knew early on they did not want to send me anywhere, but during my younger years, they didn't know what they were going to do about my education. When I was five years old, my dad received a personal call from Bob Andrews, a local attorney and one of our state representatives. Bob had introduced a bill, which had just been passed, that would provide the funding to allow students with various types of handicaps to be mainstreamed in the Gainesville City School system. This was new territory for the schools, but with the help of resource teachers provided by this new funding, I was mainstreamed, taught Braille, and other adaptations, which allowed me to be successful in a typical school environment.

Shortly after entering the first grade, I was surprised when my parents told me they had signed me up for guitar lessons and presented me with my first guitar. It was a small guitar, and at the time, my hand wouldn't even fit all the way around the neck. I really took off with the lessons. I had to toughen up my fingers, and it took me about six months to have a good grasp on the basics. The class I was in was a group class, and my mother tells a funny story that the teacher of the class relayed to her. On the day of the fourth lesson, my teacher was late to class. When she walked in, she started to tune the guitars, as was her normal practice.

"Mrs. Peters, you don't have to do that. Mark already tuned them for us," another student told her.

Mrs. Peters told my mother she checked the guitars, and they were all in tune, and she was amazed that I had done that. I do recall that experience and remember thinking that I knew I could tune my own guitar, so I figured I would just tune all the others while we waited for the teacher!

Around this same time, my parents bought the hit single "American Pie" by Don McLean for me. I remember loving the song, the melody, the chords, and the fact that it had a lot of guitar in it. "American Pie" was the first song that I really put together and could play and sing on the guitar, start to finish. I remember listening to it over and over, putting it on repeat on the little record player, many times falling asleep listening to it play.

> A long, long time ago
> I can still remember how
> That music used to make me smile
> And I knew if I had my chance
> That I could make those people dance
> and maybe they'd be happy for a while

Bye, bye Miss American Pie
Drove my Chevy to the levee but the levee was dry
Them good ole boys were drinking whiskey in Rye
Singin' this'll be the day that I die
This'll be the day that I die

So while I was growing my musical roots and discovering the wonder of being able to sing and play music, I was also just a typical little kid who loved to play in the neighborhood, getting into my fair share of trouble along the way. One of those times I remember well was in 1972 when I was six years old, and we'd learned in school about George Washington chopping down the cherry tree and confessing it to his mother. My dad worked at the local bank, which had a promotion where they gave away a dogwood tree for a $100 savings deposit. My dad ended up getting four of the prized dogwood trees, which were planted in various places around the front yard.

After hearing the story about George Washington, I remember thinking, "If it's good enough for our first president, it's good enough for me." I talked about this with my neighbor and friend Rusty, and he heartily agreed. Rusty became my partner in crime as we found a small ax, and I cut that dogwood tree down to size. I marched in the house, as proud as could be, bearing a branch off the tree, and said, "Mother, I cannot tell a lie. I chopped down the dogwood tree," thinking that my mother would surely know that I was following in the footsteps of our first president. When I walked in the house, I had it all rehearsed and wasn't even thinking about getting in trouble.

After some conversation and the appropriate tongue-lashing from my mother, Rusty was sent home, and I was sent to the living room to sit on the couch and wait for my daddy to get home and administer the real punishment. I remember him being upset over losing the dogwood, and I got a good talking-to about not bothering things that weren't mine, but I think deep down my parents were so amused that the punishment wasn't too harsh.

Chapter 2

Hope in the Dark

I mentioned that my vivid memories began around age three. All my life I have had the ability to remember dates, numbers, and details of situations, so much so that my mother calls me the family historian. I suppose part of it came from having to hold things in memory rather than writing them down. Before the days of technology and cell phones, I had to keep many phone numbers and other information in my memory bank. As far as experiences and events, I would always just relate one event to another and realized that I could remember the dates that things happened, which has proved very helpful throughout my life, especially before the advent of all the voice-recognition technology available today.

The dogwood-tree incident happened in the spring of 1972, and I'd been on the waiting list for a corneal transplant for several months at that time. Back in those days, transplant recipients were on a list and had to be ready at a moment's notice for the call to come to the hospital to receive the precious cornea. Home numbers of several family members were also given to the hospital in hopes of reaching the family as quickly as possible. It was a rainy Sunday afternoon, and we had gone to visit my aunt and uncle who lived in Atlanta. The adults were all sitting in the kitchen, and I was in the living room. The phone rang, and my aunt Doris answered it and quickly gave it to my dad.

"Okay," I heard him say. "We're on our way."

I knew immediately that call was about me, and I was excited and scared at the same time. It was a time when things were not discussed with children in detail, so nothing had really been explained to me about what would go on surrounding this surgery, and I had no idea what to expect.

Since we were already in Atlanta, it only took about twenty minutes to get to Georgia Baptist Hospital downtown. I remember arriving and getting checked into the room. The nurses came to my room to do the pre-op and administered what I would later refer to as the "I don't care" shot. I hated that shot because it made me feel "tingly" and all out of control. I remember lying there in the hospital bed just crying because it made me feel so bad. When it was time for the surgery, my dad went up in the elevator with me, all the way to a set of double doors, and that was where he said goodbye to me. I remember even as a little fellow, knowing that I was going in there alone, and just being crushed that my mother and dad weren't with me. It was cold in the operating room, and I remember them trying to warm me up with blankets. I was so agitated and fighting the mask, but they finally held me down, got the mask on, and mercifully, the anesthesia took over.

It was around midnight when I made it to recovery, and I remember being very nauseated and still agitated. They had to send for my mother to come to the recovery room, which was not normal practice because I was so out of control. I ended up pulling the stitches out, not with my hands, but I was throwing up, and was moving around so much that the stitches came loose. I remember feeling bad later about the way I had acted and that I had put everybody through that. I had to wait about a week for them to do the surgery to restitch the cornea. My eye was patched, and I remained in the hospital, but I couldn't tell any difference in my vision even during the brief times the patch was removed.

The second surgery was performed, and I was a little calmer this time, knowing more what to expect, but the "I don't care" shot still threw me for a loop, and I still had the unbearable nausea. I stayed in the hospital two more weeks, making it almost a month total that I was there. My mother was with me the entire time, and my dad made the hour-plus drive to the hospital every day, fighting the Atlanta traffic, sometimes bringing my sister with him. My sister Andrea was not allowed on the floor, but I did get to see her one time during my stay when they took me to a lobby area where she was waiting. Family and friends tried to make things as pleasant as possible, and I did receive several gifts while I was in the hospital. Sometimes it was those deliveries that kept me going, just knowing that people were thinking about me when those packages or flowers came through the door.

For the first couple of days after the surgery to restitch the cornea, I remember seeing vivid, clear images during the brief times that the patch was removed for dressing changes or when the doctor made rounds. I saw a red truck that someone had sent to me on my bed, and I remember seeing a mirror across the room, and things were very bright. This new experience was short-lived however, when the cornea started to cloud, and my world became hazy and darker once more. Things looked to me like they'd looked before, no better and no worse. I just remember being ready to go home and play; there was not any discussion of disappointment, or my feelings, or anything of the sort. People were more stoical in those days, not unhappy but just accepting what was without a lot of psychoanalysis about the experience. I think that may have been better for me at the time because I just moved on and did all the things that I wanted to do and didn't dwell on the experience or what could have been. My parents never showed their disappointment that I recall, the only reference to the surgery being some discussion of medical bills that kept coming long after the surgery had taken place.

Life for the next year was filled with all the ordinary, everyday things that centered around family, faith, and friends. Growing up in the Bible Belt, church attendance was a way of life, and my parents made sure we were at church twice on Sundays and once on Wednesday without fail. Those were the years my faith began to take root, and I remember knowing that I loved God, and He loved me back. I guess that's part of the reason I was never overwhelmed when the corneas rejected; I just knew everything was going to be okay.

Nanny Rail, my maternal grandmother, would tell me, "God has a plan for your life, and it's sure going to be a special one."

After one of my surgeries, I remember Nanny saying, "Don't you worry. God's got something for you to do that nobody else can do, and He's going to take care of you so that you'll be able to do that thing that He wants you to do."

Those precious words from Nanny and the truths I learned week in and week out at Lakewood Baptist Church were helping the spiritual roots to go deep into my soul, which would see me through both good and bad times ahead.

It was Saturday, August 26, 1972, two days before my seventh birthday, and my mother called me in from outside where I had been playing. They had just received a call from Georgia Baptist Hospital that a cornea had become available for me. Once again, our lives shifted into high gear, and we were on our way down to the hospital with a police escort that my dad arranged so we could speed without being pulled over. We arrived at Georgia Baptist in less than two hours from the time we received the call and got settled into a room. The pre-op process again included the dreaded "I don't care" shot, and once again it was a very unpleasant experience. I remember sitting in my mother's lap after the injection, with her trying to console me.

"I'm sorry we had to ask you to do this again," she said, her voice thick with emotion. It was the first time that I knew that she and my dad were really affected by everything I was having to go through. My dad again went as far with me as he could to the operating room, to the double doors, where I had to go on alone.

Once inside the OR, I had the same reaction to the mask as before. I was giving the nurses such a hard time, and finally the anesthesiologist, Dr. John Yarborough, an older doctor with a classic Southern gentleman drawl, said from across the room, "Why doncha let him administa the anesthesia?"

"What do you mean?" said the nurse, surprised.

"Let 'im hold the mask," said Dr. Yarborough.

"We've never done that before," she said.

To which, he replied, "Well, there's a first time for everything." Then he turned to me and said, "Do you want to pretend like you're an astronaut?"

"Yeah," I said through my tears and with a shaky voice.

They handed me the mask, and with only slight hesitation, I put it over my nose and mouth.

"Breathe real deep now so you can get out into space fasta," was the last thing I remember hearing from the anesthesiologist.

The surgery itself went well, and once again we played the waiting game to see if my body would accept or reject the cornea. I was in the hospital for two weeks this time, and my birthday was two days after the surgery. Not knowing that I would be in the hospital, a big birthday party had already been planned for my seventh birthday. Of course, it had to be cancelled, but they had a party for me in the hospital instead, and several friends of the family came to help me celebrate.

My doctor, JC Lester, had made rounds that morning and found out it was my birthday. When he came back for evening rounds, he made sure he rounded during the time of my party. He had gone to the Milton Bradley Toy Store that afternoon and told them he needed the biggest fire truck they had. He presented me with the gift, and I couldn't believe he would do that for me. Dr. Lester had done the previous surgery as well, and we seemed to have a special bond that would grow through the years.

The times when the patch was off briefly, I remember seeing the toys and flowers in my room. Colors were more vivid, and images were sharper, and this continued throughout my time in the hospital. With each day that passed, it appeared that this time would be different, that the cornea was going to "take." I enjoyed several weeks of this increased visual acuity and had been back at school about a week when I noticed a clouding starting at the top of my eye. Over the course of the next two days, the cloudiness continued to spread from the top down, until my whole visual field was cloudy. I told my parents, and they made an appointment for Dr. Lester to see me in his office.

In Dr. Lester's office, he looked at the cornea and said, "Yes, I'm sorry to say, it has rejected." There was no crying or talk of disappointment—just the solid acceptance of what was: my body had rejected this cornea as well. At that point, we took a step back and decided to take some time off from trying another transplant. I remember I just wanted to be a normal kid.

Chapter 3

THREADING THE NEEDLE

Not long after the failed transplant, I told my parents I wanted to learn to ride a bike. I started practicing on Andrea's old blue-and-white bike that had training wheels on it. My dad put the training wheels on the ground at first and kept moving them up so I would have to learn to balance more and more. I got the knack of it fairly quickly by riding on the driveway. One day I came out to ride, and the training wheels were off the bike.

I went to my dad and asked, "Where are the training wheels?"

"I took them off because I thought you could balance well enough that you didn't need them anymore," he said.

I was surprised, and I asked him to come help me as I tried it for the first time. I rode down the driveway with my dad running beside me. Everything was going fine until I made the turn at the end of the driveway too sharp and wiped out. I got back up and got on again, mad that I had fallen. I went down the driveway again, and this time, I knew what I had to do to keep my balance in the turn. That was just one of many experiences where my parents let me try my wings and weren't afraid to see me possibly fail, fall, and then try again.

The Christmas of '72, I received as a gift my own orange-and-black bike. I gained more confidence with that bike and was soon riding other places besides our driveway with speed and risk taking, which sometimes caused my mother and dad to watch me with their hands over their eyes, praying I would make it. Most of those times occurred when my dad would whistle, which was the signal to come home for supper. From my neighbor's house two doors away, it was all downhill. I could work up a lot of speed as I went, and by the time I got to the driveway next to ours, I was going at a pretty good clip. I remember the feel of the wind going through my hair and around my ears, and for me, it was absolute freedom.

The last part of the journey, I would go through our yard and onto the driveway. The scary part for my parents was that we had many large trees in our yard, some of which were very close together. I couldn't see those trees until I was right up on them, which would have been much too late to stop. For me, it was like threading a needle, and somehow I went through with precision every time. I had walked and ridden the path so many times before that I knew where every tree was and what I had to do to go between them. Miraculously, I never fell or hit a tree going through the yard, but sometimes I would be going so fast that I would end up running into the bumper of my dad's car in the driveway.

The same Christmas that I received the bike, Andrea and I received together a basketball goal as a gift from my parents. Earlier that year, my mother started taking Andrea and me to the park. Andrea was already becoming a good tennis player and would hit tennis balls while my mother taught me how to shoot baskets. We would play "horse," and I had a surprising amount of accuracy, given the fact that the backboard and rim were very indistinct at that point. When we got the new basketball goal for the driveway, I spent a lot of time honing my skills even more.

One of the board members on the board of directors at Home Federal, the bank where my dad would spend thirty-five years working in various positions, told my dad at a board meeting one morning, "I drove by your house the other day and saw Mark out there shooting baskets. I just stopped the car and watched him for a few minutes, and he hit nearly every one of them!" Some people who knew us and would drive by and see me out there would tell my parents they nearly had a wreck trying to drive and watch me shoot baskets at the same time.

So while I was gaining more confidence and learning new things, I also had my first opportunities to play the guitar and sing in public in 1972. I was asked to play at the Fair Street Middle School

Christmas program. They had asked me to sing "Silent Night," and it was the first time I played an electric guitar. I brought my acoustic guitar, but since they did not have a way to mic it, they asked if I would play the electric guitar they had on hand. They explained that the electric guitar had amplification, which would be needed if the guitar were to be heard in the gym. I picked up the electric guitar and immediately fell in love with the sound. I didn't know at the time that my parents already had an electric guitar for me for Christmas.

It was during my second-grade year that people started asking me to bring my guitar to school to sing and play. Several times, my teacher would devote time for me to sing and play for the whole class. I remember the students would get quiet and really tune in and listen. The more I played, the more they liked it, and the more it motivated me to play and get better. I began to realize the guitar was a great way to make friends and be accepted. I had never been shy, but by this time, when the guitar was in my hands, I went from the sometimes awkward "blind kid" in the class to that "cool kid" that everybody wanted to be around. I wasn't afraid to play—all they had to do was ask.

Chapter 4

New York State of Mind

As far as my vision, I continued to go back to Dr. Lester to be seen and assessed throughout the year. They were doing more to try and decrease the chances of further rejection, or rejection of future transplants. I was on even more cortisone and gained a lot of weight. I had that "moon pie" face that's sometimes associated with steroids. Even after a cornea had started to reject, it was thought that further rejection could be stopped, and the process sometimes reversed with increased steroids. Dr. Lester always tried to be optimistic about the transplants and what was going on with me. For most of 1972–73, I had gone to Dr. Lester's office, sometimes once a week, for the cortisone injections. Sometime in the summer of 1973, it was decided in Dr. Lester's office that we would attempt another transplant. Again we were put on a waiting list for the cornea and had to be sitting on ready for the call.

On Wednesday, August 8, 1973, around noon, the call we were waiting for came, and we went back to Georgia Baptist Hospital to receive another cornea that had just become available. At that point, as a seven-year-old, I didn't realize that in order for me to get a cornea, it meant that someone had died and donated it. This was never told to me as a child, and I never came to that realization until much later. The drill for the surgery was the same: we had a police escort to get there as quickly as possible and arrived in less than two hours from the initial call. Once in the room, the nurses came to give the "I don't care" shot.

"I don't want the shot," I said boldly.

One of the nurses protested and tried her best to get me to take it.

"Have you ever had one of those shots?" I asked her.

"No," she said.

"Well, I have, and I don't like the way it makes me feel, and I'm not going to take it."

"I'll have to check with the anesthesiologist," she said. (It was the same anesthesiologist from the previous surgeries).

She came back with the information that they would not require me to take the shot. So they took me on to surgery, with my dad again by my side, until I passed through the doors. Once in the operating room, Dr. Yarborough greeted me and handed me the mask, like I was the old pro at that point. The surgery again appeared to go well, and the recovery process in the hospital was easier this time. As the patch was taken off, periodically in the hospital, though, my vision lacked the clarity I had experienced with the previous surgery; I believe that it had already rejected even before the patch was taken off the first time. There were some funny moments, however, during my hospital stay and recovery.

A couple of Dad's friends from work, Roger Bower and Warren Blackman, who were young bachelors, both with a great sense of humor, came to stay with me one night so Mom and Dad could go out to dinner. For a gift, they brought me one of those bearskin rugs with the bear head attached to it that were popular then. Roger and Warren decided they wanted to play a trick on the nurses with that rug, so we walked to the nurses' station; and while one of them distracted the nurses, I put the rug on top of my head so that the head of the bear was looking over the top of the counter. The nurse turned around and gave a little yell and sort of backed up, according to the guys. I stood up to show her I was under the rug, and everyone had a good laugh about that. On the same night, Roger and Warren thought it would be fun to have wheelchair races down the hall. They put me in one of the chairs, and Roger pushed me while Warren was in the other chair, going as fast as he could. We got a couple of good races in, going full throttle to the elevators and back, before the nurses discovered us and told the boys to get me back to my room and into bed.

Another thing I remember about that time was that I was awake more, being older, and I was easily bored during the recovery process.

I asked my dad to bring my guitar to the hospital, which he did. I was playing one night, and I started playing and singing "Amazing Grace." Before I knew it, people had started to gather outside my door: nurses, other patients, and people just walking by. They clapped when I finished, and so I sang another one! I was discovering more and more that I had the ability to make people happy with my music, and that was an amazing feeling as an eight-year-old kid.

We left the hospital, with my vision basically no better and no worse than when I came in. We went home and got back into the routine of life without skipping a beat. I was out of the hospital in time to have a real "kid" birthday party that year but was still considered to be in the recovery process, so I was two weeks later than my classmates starting back to school.

In September, I went back to Dr. Lester's office for a post-op visit. I arrived midafternoon and had to wait a long time for him to see me that day. Others who got there after me were being seen, and we wondered why they didn't call us back. We were the last ones in the waiting room and were finally shown to a room. Dr. Lester came in and examined me and, after he had finished, said, "Wait right there. I'll be right back." He went out of the room and was gone just a few seconds. He came back into the room holding something behind his back. "By golly, I missed your birthday this year! I remembered it was on August 28, and you weren't anywhere around here then. When I knew you were coming in today, I thought I'd bring you this," he said as he brought the beautiful instrument out from behind his back. It was a fine banjo, with a resonator that was a sparkly red color and a glossy natural-colored neck. "Wow, wow, wow, thank you, thank you, thank you!" I stammered. I had tried to play a banjo before, and I tried again right there in the office and did manage to make a little sound with it. I still have that banjo today.

So far, my body had rejected five corneas, three in the right eye and two in the left. It seemed that the traditional cornea transplant was just not going to work for me since my body fought off each cornea like a foreign invader. Following the fifth failed transplant, Dr. Lester suggested that we try a cutting-edge new procedure that had just been developed by a doctor in Spain. Only a handful of patients at that time had been recipients of the Cardona keratoprosthesis, basically an artificial cornea that was restoring vision for people for whom the traditional cornea transplant had failed. Dr. Hernando Cardona from Spain developed the procedure and had flown all over the world performing the surgery in various countries, with promising results.

In the spring of 1974, my parents, sister, and I traveled to Columbia Presbyterian Hospital in New York for me to have a preliminary assessment and workup to see if I would be a candidate for this procedure. It was the week of spring break, and we spent four days in New York City. The time spent in the doctor's office was only about one hour, and the rest of the time we spent touring. We went to the top of Empire State Building, climbed the Statue of Liberty, visited Chinatown, Little Italy, and my personal favorite, FAO Schwartz. From there, we traveled to Washington, DC, on a Greyhound bus, which took about four hours. We took in the sights and visited the White House, the Washington Monument, the Lincoln and Jefferson Memorials, the Smithsonian Air and Space Museum, FBI headquarters, and the Bureau of Printing and Engraving.

After a week of nonstop activity, we went home and waited on the word from New York as to whether this new surgery was even a possibility. It was April 8, 1974, and my mother had just picked my sister and me up from school. The weather report was on the radio, and there was a chance of afternoon thunderstorms. About thirty minutes after we got home, however, things started to get dicey with the weather. Gainesville, Georgia, seems to be a magnet for tornados, the whole town having been destroyed by one in 1936. The '36 tornado was part of the second-worst tornado outbreak in recorded US history, taking 203 lives in Gainesville alone, so we were always on the alert when bad weather was imminent.

Mother sent Andrea and me to the basement while she watched the skies out the window. We stayed there for about five seconds, deciding that we needed to see what was going on too. Then we heard something that sounded like a train. I had always heard that a tornado sounded like a train, but nothing could have prepared me for that sound, or the terror I felt, as we knew it was getting closer.

The awful sound got louder and louder, and we followed Mother from room to room in the house, watching the destruction outside, not sure what was going to happen next. The tornado came right over our house, uprooting trees in its wake. The whole thing only took about one minute, but I had never been that scared in my life and really thought we might die. As it turned out, there was very little damage to the house, but the yard was completely torn up: the tornado had downed twelve large pine trees in our yard alone and had done damage to many houses around us. My dad, attempting to make his way home from the bank following the storm, couldn't even drive all the way home because of all the trees and debris on the road. He had to stop about a mile from the house and walk the rest of the way. It didn't take long after it was over, however, for people to come outside, with chain saws and other equipment to begin the cleanup process, neighbors helping neighbors, as was always the case in our close-knit community.

Everyone was outside, and I heard the phone ringing in the house. I went and answered it, and on the line was the doctor from New York. He asked to speak to my mom or dad, so my mom went to the phone and learned the good news that I was, in fact, a candidate for the ground-breaking surgery. In order for me to receive this artificial cornea, the cornea and lens from my right eye would have to be removed. Plans were made immediately for Dr. Lester to remove the cornea and lens, which he did, in two surgeries, five days apart in June of 1974.

A couple of months after the surgeries to remove the cornea and lens, we were on a plane back to Columbia Presbyterian Hospital for the procedure to implant the keratoprosthesis. We had a 6:00 a.m. flight and had to be at the airport at 4:30 a.m. It was a challenge trying to get to the airport that early, so in the interest of time, my dad was going to have the valet at the airport park the car in one of the extended stay lots for us. We pulled up and got out of the car in the appropriate place for the valet parking. There was only one problem—when we exited the car, my dad put the keys in his pocket instead of leaving them in the ignition. It was not until we were on the plane that he reached his hand in his pocket, felt the cold metal of the keys, and came to the realization that he had left his car on the curb, and the valet would have no way to move it. When we arrived at the airport in New York, he placed a call to the Atlanta airport and learned the car had been towed. However, when the airport officials learned our situation, the towing fee was waived, and we just had to call when we got back to have it brought up from the impound lot.

We arrived in New York on Monday morning and, by Monday afternoon, were going through all the pre-op procedures in Dr. Gerald DeVoe's office. My surgery was scheduled for early afternoon the next day. My parents had briefed this new surgical team on my need to place the mask over my nose and mouth myself and the fact that I didn't want the "I don't care" shot before being taken to the OR, so I was hoping I wouldn't have any trouble from the adults with either of those things. The operating room at Columbia Presbyterian Hospital was different from the large one at Georgia Baptist. It was small, about the size of a large master bedroom, and it actually had a window in it. I had not met Dr. Cardona until the day of the surgery, and he greeted me in broken English in the operating room. I was excited and nervous and, at their direction, took the mask in hand and was soon out.

The next morning, Dr. DeVoe was ready to see me in his office. His office was attached to the hospital, and I went in a wheelchair through the hospital to the office. Dr. DeVoe took the patch off, and immediately I was able to see across the room. I remember seeing my mother, seeing her face clearly.

I thought, "Wow, I can't believe this. I never thought I'd be able to see this well."

Dr. DeVoe was pleased and told me I could keep the patch off during the day and was only required to wear it at night while I slept, which was very different from the previous surgeries. We went back to the room and, over the next couple of days, spent a lot of time walking around the hospital, looking out of windows. There was a window that looked out over the Hudson Bay, and I was able to see boats on the water from that window. I was awake and alert following this surgery like I'd never been after the others. Friday came, and they told us we could go home, which was really different from the fourteen-day stays typical of the previous surgeries.

By Friday morning, I began to notice a slight change, a little clouding in my vision, but I figured it was just settling down a bit, and it was still a tremendous improvement over what I had before. We made the flight home, and after we got the situation with the car sorted out, we went by Dr. Lester's office. The office was closed, but Dr. Lester had wanted to see me, so he met us at the office, along with one of his assistants that we had come to know well through the years. Dr. Lester was blown away with the result and felt like the surgery was a complete success—the success we'd waited on for years. I was anxious to get home, to see my family and all my surroundings. We stopped at my Granny Dowdy's house (my father's mother) to pick up Andrea and then went to Nanny Rail's house so that they could see me; and I, with more clarity than ever before, could see them.

I was contented to be home, and the next morning when I came downstairs, my mother said, "You'd better go ahead and get your breakfast because we've got a surprise for you." I ate hurriedly in suspense about what the surprise could be. Within a half hour, a big delivery truck pulled up in our driveway from a local music store that I frequented as often as my parents would let me. I was shocked when they started to unload the big double-keyboard organ that I had played for literally hours in their store in the local mall. The men got it all set up, and I played and played all day long; it was definitely the most professional instrument I'd had to that point. People kept coming by to see me after the surgery, and I'd play for anybody who came in. I was almost more excited about that keyboard than I was about the successful surgery and my increased vision!

I was able to start school on time with everyone else that year. The increase in my visual acuity came with some big changes for me in the way I did my schoolwork. I continued to use braille for a significant amount of my work, but now I was able read large print, so most of my math problems I was now able to do on paper. I used big sheets of blank newsprint paper, and I would spread the paper on the floor in the back of the classroom and was able to do my problems that way. My confidence level increased even more with my increase in vision as I experienced the world around me as never before.

Chapter 5

SEEING THE LIGHT

In August of 1975, I began to sense what I would describe as God tugging at my heart, not just in church but during my daily activities. I had a sense that He was with me and wanted me to follow Him in a deeper way than I had before. I felt like something was unsettled that needed to be settled. I talked to my parents about this, and they had our pastor, Al Craft, come talk to me on an August day just before my tenth birthday. He told me about God's love that afternoon, the same sweet story I'd heard so many times before. We talked about sin and how none of us is perfect but that it is important to live a life and do things that are pleasing to God. He asked me if I knew that asking Jesus into my heart meant that I would spend eternity in heaven with him. I said I did, and I knew and understood all that we talked about as much as an almost ten-year-old can. We prayed that day, and I put the spiritual stake in the ground that marked the beginning of my journey, my walk with God. I was baptized on a cool, rainy day in September of that year by Pastor Craft at Lakewood Baptist Church. My grandparents, aunts, uncles, cousins, and friends were all there, and we had a celebration at our house following the service. This spiritual marker would be something I would look back on many times and is part of what would sustain me in the dark times ahead.

It was December 1975, and I had passed the year mark of having my artificial cornea, an important milestone for any transplant recipient in terms of acceptance or rejection. My new vision had allowed me to see things and do things that I never thought I would. I still remember where the sun was in the sky the day my world changed.

I was in the fifth grade, and we were outside for our second recess of the day. Some girls had been on the swings for a long time and had just moved off and on to some other activity. My friends and I had been waiting for the swings, so we eagerly clambered over to claim a swing for ourselves. Deciding she wasn't finished swinging after all, one girl came back and demanded that I let her have the swing. I held my ground and refused to give in.

"You got off the swing, and you'd been on it a long time," I said.

As I remember, she was not a girl who was normally mean; but this time, she let her emotions get away from her, and she punched me. The punch landed on my right eye. It really hurt, but not noticing any change in vision, I didn't really think much about it after that.

Several days later, our family was getting ready to go to the lighting of the Christmas tree at our local mall. I had noticed that afternoon that my vision seemed to be getting dimmer. As the hours went by, it got darker and darker; and by the time we left for the Christmas-tree lighting, it was all but gone. I didn't say anything about it that night, thinking it would come back in the morning. I guess that's how a ten-year-old's mind works. The next morning, it was just the same, dark and dull. I told my parents, and they immediately called Dr. Lester's office. He scheduled an appointment for me to see a retina specialist. In the meantime, though, I went to school, and I remember having trouble as I walked into the classroom and being confused with the rows of desks. I also had to sing for a Lion's Club Christmas luncheon that day, so life went on.

The next day, however, I was in Atlanta, spending the day being assessed by the retina specialist. In looking for the cause of the detached retina, the playground incident was the only trauma I had experienced, and the doctor said it was likely the cause of my problem. The retina had torn and detached slowly as the days passed that week. He recommended that we go back to New York and see Dr. DeVoe because they had a machine called a B scan that could see with greater clarity in the back of the eye, and there was not one in Atlanta. We made plans to go back to New York a week to the day of my initial complaint.

The next day, I came in from school and collapsed in the recliner. Sometimes after school, I would stretch out there and take a short nap. I remember this day being hit with a wave of depression, and I just broke down and cried, and thought, *Why did this have to happen?* It didn't take long, however, for me to pull myself together and get ready for the trip. We arrived in New York, and the scan was performed. We sat in Dr. DeVoe's office, me on my father's lap, my mother beside us

"It's not the news you want to hear, but your retina is detached, and it is a complete detachment. There's a possibility that it can be fixed, but these surgeries are rarely successful." He was always very matter-of-fact, not unkind but just stating it the way it was. I remember again just breaking down and crying at the news. Once that moment was over, though, I had the resolve that I needed to move on. I was ready to get on with the surgery to try the reattachment, but I knew I'd be okay even if it didn't work. The roots of my faith may have been young and tender, but they were strong enough to hold me. Christmas was coming, and life was good, and I was ready to get back into it.

I was excited about getting to fly home on an L-1011 because I had never flown on a plane that size before. It was smooth sailing until we reached Atlanta. We were coming in for the landing, the runway visible below, wheels ready to touch down. Then all of a sudden, the plane went straight back up into the air. The vibration was intense, like the plane was going to break apart. The lights in cabin went almost dark, presumably because the engines were pulling so much power to get us back up in the air. Soon we leveled off, and the shaking stopped, but we were scared because we didn't know what was going on.

The pilot's calm voice soon came on the radio, "Ladies and gentlemen, sorry about that. It seems another plane was taking off on the wrong runway, and we almost landed on top of them. Everything is okay. We're just circling around Chattanooga and should be back to Atlanta in about ten minutes," he said. We did land without further incident, and my parents and I headed back to Gainesville.

The surgery to attempt to reattach my retina was scheduled for January 2, 1976. I went into the hospital on New Year's Day, and Dr. Lester came by that evening to meet with us. The surgery was done the following morning at a new hospital in Atlanta called Metropolitan Hospital, a hospital treating eye, ear, nose, and throat disorders. By this time, I really was an old pro at the surgeries. I was still nervous, but I could handle it, so there was not the drama of the earlier surgeries. In recovery from the procedure, they wanted me to stay mainly on my stomach, with my head turned to the right so as not to put pressure on the right eye. While recovering, I spent a lot of time in the prone position, just sleeping. I was in the hospital for about a week, but when the patch would come off for dressing changes, or for me to be examined, I didn't notice any change in my vision whatsoever—there was still just darkness.

It would be several weeks later in Dr. Lester's office that he would examine me and say with certainty that the surgery had not been successful. Dr. Lester was distressed that the surgery had failed; he had an excellent reputation in the Atlanta area and had performed many successful transplant and retina-repair surgeries. I think it was particularly distressing to him since, for some reason, he seemed to have taken a special interest in me and was clearly doing all he could to make sure I had the best shot possible at increasing my vision.

Dr. Lester had heard of a cutting-edge procedure for retinal detachment that was being performed by Dr. MacKenzie Freeman, an eye specialist at Boston Mass General. The procedure involved an inverted operating table which put the retina in the position to determine more about its viability. He wanted me to go to Boston and meet with Dr. Freeman to see about making one last attempt to reattach the retina and save my eye.

Oh no, not another surgery, I thought, but plans were soon made for us to make the trip. Again my parents and I boarded a plane in Atlanta and were off to Boston a few days early so the doctors could meet with us before the surgery. We arrived on a Thursday night. It was snowing, so much so that the plane had to be towed in once we landed. We met with Dr. Freeman for him to evaluate me on Friday morning. He said the surgery was a go and thought he could get good results. I also had to be assessed and cleared for surgery by a local pediatrician. His name was Dr. Gantz, and he was quite an unusual man, probably in his late seventies. We walked in the office, and my parents said it looked like something from the 1920s.

We soon learned, however, that Dr. Gantz was world-renowned and had treated the likes of the Kennedy children, and sometimes the children of foreign dignitaries who would come to the US. Dr. Gantz, of course, knew we were from Georgia. Jimmy Carter was running for president, but it was before the time that he was very well known outside of our area. But Dr. Gantz seemed to know all about him and kept making jokes about the "peanut farmer" from Georgia. After Jimmy Carter was elected, we sent Dr. Gantz a letter stating that since the "peanut farmer" was now our president, we thought he might like to have a bag of Georgia Peanuts. We received a nice letter back thanking us for sending those prized peanuts and telling us how much he had enjoyed meeting us.

Over the weekend, we took in the sights and sounds of Boston. I enjoyed one last meal at Friendly's, and then it was time to get to the hospital to prepare for the surgery on Monday. We walked several blocks in the snow from the hotel to the hospital that afternoon. The following morning was cold and gray. I remember on the news there was the story of a fellow who had jumped from a bridge close by that morning, and everyone was talking about it. Local people said there had been several suicides lately. The economy was bad, and people were having a hard time finding work. Several had jumped to their deaths down into the freezing water off this particular bridge.

I was slightly nervous but hopeful about the surgery. The surgical team was good and knew all my special "requirements" to make the situation more tolerable for me. I guess they could look back and see how many surgeries I'd had before (this was number twelve), so they could trust me to know what I needed. The surgery took approximately eight hours, and at least some of that time, I was on the inverted operating table. I don't have any recollection of anything until the next evening when the patch came off for a dressing change. I didn't notice any change in vision, still the same darkness that I was now growing accustomed to. I remember thinking that maybe it was healing, and there was still some hope that it would change.

We had a visitor that did brighten our spirits while we were in Boston. A friend of my dad's, Dr. Scott Cunningham, then a professor at Harvard, came for a visit that Monday. He and my dad had been in service together and had a close friendship. There were no televisions or radios in patient rooms in the hospital, and Scott took notice of that. The following day, a small television and radio were delivered to our room, courtesy of Scott Cunningham. That really helped to pass the time while we were there and was one of those kindnesses that you don't soon forget.

I stayed in the hospital about two weeks, and each time the patch came off, I sensed no change in my vision. It was the last night before I was to go home, and I was taken to Dr. Freeman's office, which was attached to the hospital. I remember lying on the table for him to examine me. He looked in my eye and said, "No, it didn't work." I wasn't surprised but felt let down just the same. I heard what I knew already but was hoping to hear something else. Dr. Freeman went out of the room and into another patient's room. With walls being thin, I could hear some of his conversation with that patient, who also had a detached retina. He was an older man, and his surgery had been successful, but he was upset with Dr. Freeman about something. Dr. Freeman came back into our room with final instructions. As we were saying our goodbyes, he expressed his regret that the surgery had not been successful.

"It's so sad. This surgery didn't work, and this young man has his whole life in front of him, with so much promise. The man in the next room—his surgery was a success, and he doesn't even appreciate what he's got," he said, his voice filled with sadness.

Once again, though, the resolve that I was going to make it came over me, and I was ready to get back home, so ready. My dad had gone back to Georgia because he had to get back to work. My mother and I boarded a plane for home, our last hope of recovering any vision in my right eye *gone*.

It was after we returned home that my parents told me it would be my decision if any more surgeries were to be done after that point.

They knew how much I had been through, and they didn't want to put me through any more unless it was my choice to do it. I remember feeling happy and relieved to hear them say that. I was ready to be done with surgeries and couldn't envision a scenario where I'd want to have any more transplant surgeries to my remaining eye, in which I did have some light perception.

I went back to school a couple of weeks after returning home, without the vision that I'd become accustomed to and grown to depend on. I returned to doing all my work in braille, no longer being able to see well enough to do my math problems on paper. It seemed, however, that I soon adjusted and adapted to using what little vision and light perception I had in my left eye. I honestly never had any harsh feelings toward the girl that had punched me and caused all this to happen. Looking back now as an adult, I can see how the seeds of bitterness could have easily been sown, but that just wasn't my ten-year-old way of looking at things. I was glad to be back at school and get back into life—a life that I knew was still worth living.

All the surgeries of the past several years had stretched my parents financially to the breaking point. While my dad had good insurance with his position at the bank, there was still a significant portion of each surgery that my family had to pay out of pocket. In fact, for the hospital in Boston, the insurance only paid about 10 percent of the total cost. The room alone was approximately $250 per day, a significant amount at that time. Besides the medical costs, there were all the costs of plane tickets and travel for three people for multiple trips to New York and the one trip to Boston. Sometimes my dad had to stay in a hotel while my mother stayed with me. Once he was allowed to stay in the intern quarters at Columbia Presbyterian for a cost of $30 for the entire time he was there.

After the twelfth surgery, my dad went to a local banker friend at First National Bank in Gainesville to see about consolidating some of the debt he was paying on associated with the medical bills. The friend was willing to make the loan and told my dad that there would be a line of credit for all he needed to pay off the existing bills and that it could be drawn on as he needed it for future expenses. He told my dad, "Just sign the note, and you can pay it back whenever you can, however you want to." My dad recalls the interest rate being very low as well. My parents paid on the loan for several years and were thankful for the day they had paid off the debt and could close the line of credit. Back in those days, banking was done many times on a handshake and a man's good name, and my father certainly had a good name in our community.

Chapter 6

WINGS TO FLY

It was the spring of the year in 1976, and I felt like I had adapted well to the loss of vision I had experienced a few months earlier. I still did most of the activities I did before, just sometimes in a different way. I rode my bike, but I never rode on the street after I had the detached retina. I still rode in the yard and between the trees, but just not as fast. I got more cautious after that. My friends and I would play a new game we called *street surfing*. We would attach a rope to a bike and a skateboard, and I would balance on the skateboard as they pulled it along with the bike. That way, I could enjoy the speed without having to be the one "driving." In March, I remember feeling very hopeful as spring arrived, bringing warmer weather and brighter days. I felt like I'd made it through the long, dark winter, and just like the trees were starting to blossom, my spirit was awakening as well.

It was the beginning of what I would call my "breakout" year musically. It all started with a restaurant in Oakwood, Georgia, called the Snack Shack. The owner of the restaurant, Sonny Allegro, was well known in town, and his children went to school with my sister. He had a keyboard and sound system in the restaurant, and he himself would sing and play for the entertainment of the patrons. One Saturday night, our family had gone to enjoy some pizza, and he saw me in the crowd. He came over and asked if I'd like to sing a song.

"Do you know 'I Write the Songs'?" he asked.

"Yes," I said, which really stretched the truth since I had never sung the song, but I had heard it on the radio several times.

I wanted to sing, though, so I went to the front and stood there while he played the introduction. Somehow I was able to sing that song and recall every word without a hitch. There was a full house that night, and they seemed to love it. The applause was really loud, and they wanted me to sing another one. I sang several more, and by the end of the night, Sonny asked me if I wanted to come back and "headline" and do a whole program myself.

"Sure!" I answered, excited for the opportunity.

The next time I played, it was just me and the guitar. He paid me $100 to come and play that night.

I was in the fifth grade, and I remember thinking, *I didn't know you could get paid this much for something you just love to do!*

It was around this time that Barbara Shirley, a community leader and advocate for the visually impaired, contacted my parents about me singing at Habersham County's Kind-O-Country spectacular. She had heard about me and wanted me to come sing at the festival in April. The *Gainesville Times*, our local newspaper, heard about my involvement in the festival and did an article about me. The Habersham paper featured me in an article as well. I gained some notoriety from the articles and performing at the festival itself, and soon I had four or five bookings in a row. I sang at several events where I actually made money, again being amazed people would pay me for doing something that I loved to do and that apparently made others happy as well.

Sonny called me back to do a program with him at the pizza place, where the two of us sang and played together, and this time he paid me $150! After the articles came out and before the festival, my teacher asked me to bring my guitar to school. I spent the day going to every class in the school, singing and playing songs I planned to sing in the program. One of the bigger events I did that fall was the Northeast Georgia Mountain Fair in Clarkesville, Georgia. I was on the big stage at that event and did the opening night and the closing night. So all these things were helping lift my spirits, and I knew somehow that through my music, I was in turn helping to lift the spirits of others. I always realized that my ability was a gift, a gift that God had given me. Again I was amazed at the doors music seemed to open and the barriers it was breaking down for me in my life as I met the challenges each day brought.

In May of 1976, in the midst of all the exciting things happening with my music, another eye surgery, my thirteenth, was required to remove the keratoprosthesis from my right eye. My eye had begun to atrophy after the detached retina, and it was determined by Dr. Lester that the keratoprosthesis needed to be removed. I went in Metropolitan Hospital on Friday afternoon for the surgery and was able to go home Sunday morning.

I continued to see Dr. Lester for post-op and for management of my left eye over the next few months. During an office visit in September of that year, Dr. Lester talked to us about the idea of a prosthesis for the right eye. My eye, in addition to being atrophied, had begun to stay closed all the time, and I was losing the ability to open it. Having a prosthesis would allow my eye to stay open and hopefully preserve the musculature responsible for moving the eye within the socket. Dr. Lester happened to have a prosthesis in his office that day and popped it in my eye. It went right in, and I sensed no discomfort from it. The prosthesis was not completely round but a shell that covered my eye, which was shrunken and caved in looking at that point.

I got my prosthesis in October, and it was a five- to six-hour process of actually making it to fit my eye. I had to sit with a mold in my eye, not blinking, for quite a while, which was very uncomfortable. Driving in to the hospital that day, we had seen Dr. Lester's helicopter in the parking lot. He was an avid pilot and used his helicopter each day to fly in from his farm in Snellville, Georgia, and beat the Atlanta traffic. We went to the desk to ask them to page him and learned he was in surgery at that time. He contacted us later in the day with a time to meet up with us and show us the helicopter. I sat in the pilot's seat and was amazed at the instrumentation and that he got to fly that helicopter every day. He wanted to take me up, but my parents were hesitant to let me go. I guess they trusted Dr. Lester with my life in the OR, just not in a helicopter!

We went back to the office to get my prosthesis. It fit well, and I was glad to have something that would help my eye to stay open and look more "normal." I soon learned too that the prosthesis was a good conversation piece in a weird sort of way. I remember I used to take it out in art class at the insistence of my friends, and we'd spin it around on the art able. Looking back now, it probably wasn't the most hygienic thing to be doing with something that you take in and out of your eye socket, but eleven-year-old boys don't think about things like that.

One thing I was thinking about, though, was how difficult school was that year. I had "graduated" from elementary school with the end of fifth grade, and sixth grade was the beginning of middle school, with a whole new building, as well as a new set of expectations. Math got more complex, and there was a lot more "note-taking" that was required. I took notes with a braille machine, which was quite loud, although there were pads that I used designed to dampen the sound. If it ever distracted anyone, they never complained about it, but I don't see how it could not have been a distraction for the other students.

Taking notes with the braille typewriter was a very slow process, and I couldn't always keep up with the pace of the lecturer. Socially, I made friends easily, which was a good thing because it was not just the same crowd from elementary school but students who came to the middle school from several feeder schools. So while I was trying to "hang on" academically, I was enjoying new friendships, once again the music helping me to overcome the awkwardness that could have kept me in the shadows.

It was in the fall of my sixth grade year that I sang my first solo in church. I had done a lot of singing in the community at that point, but I had never been asked to sing in church. Children did not typically sing in the worship service unless it was one of the children's choirs, so I was surprised when our minister of music asked me to sing. I sang "Precious Lord, Take My Hand," and Della Ruth Johnson, our church organist, accompanied me. I remember standing behind the podium feeling fairly secure with it in front of me. I was used to playing while I sang, so it was a different experience to not have something to hold on to. Della Ruth, an excellent musician and a fine lady in our community, took a special interest in showing me all about the organ in the sanctuary. She would have me sit on the bench, and she would show me all the stops and pedals and the function of each one.

"You may need to know this one day," she'd say to me.

As it turned out, I did play that organ a short time later for Youth Day on a Sunday morning. I remember being just as comfortable singing "Precious Lord, Take My Hand," as I was singing the popular songs of the day, and enjoyed being able to sing for the people in my church as well.

It was in my sixth grade year that I had one of the most thrilling experiences of my young life. Early in 1975, I had begun to listen to John Denver and fell in love with his music. It was an era when top 40 radio played different genres of music side by side, so it exposed people to various styles of music that were popular at the time. I remember hearing John Denver songs like "Annie's Song" (You Fill Up My Senses), and "Country Road." His songs always had such great melodies, and it was easy to make them sound good with just a guitar and voice. In 1976, my dad bought the 8-track for me of John Denver's "live" album. I nearly wore the tape out listening to songs like "Thank God I'm a Country Boy," "Today," and "The Eagle and the Hawk," to name a few. The one song I probably loved the most was "Poems, Prayers and Promises." It had such a beautiful, singable melody, and I loved the lyrics:

> We talk of poems, prayers and promises
> Things that we believe in
> How sweet it is to love someone
> How right it is to care
> How long it's been since yesterday
> and what about tomorrow
> What about our dreams
> and all the memories we've shared…

I've been lately thinking
About my life's time
All the things I've done
And how it's been
And I can't help believing
In my own mind
I know I'm gonna hate to see it end

One day my dad received a call from his old friend Scott Cunningham, who had been appointed to the National Education Foundation Board by President Ford. It just so happened that John Denver was also on the NEF Board. Scott told my dad that John Denver was going to be in Atlanta and asked if we wanted tickets and backstage passes so that I could meet John Denver. Of course, my dad said yes! And it was all arranged through John Denver's office. We had great seats on the floor at the concert, right beside the mixing console.

The guy that announced, "Ladies and gentleman—welcome John Denver," was the same one that I'd listened to over and over on the 8-track live album.

I was sitting an arm's length from him, and I couldn't believe it! In the concert, John Denver sang all the songs I'd come to love so well and had listened to over and over, songs that had brought me so much joy.

Even sitting there as an eleven-year-old, I remember thinking, *I'd love to be up there doing that!*

All too soon, the concert was over, and we waited a long time for them to come get us and take us backstage. We went through what seemed like a maze to get to the place where he was. We waited only a few minutes, and out came John Denver. He was very friendly and shook my hand.

"I love your music, and I sing a lot of your songs," I told him.

I remember his phrase of the day was "far out," and he answered me with a, "Far out, man!"

He was full of life, in his prime at thirty-one years old, and bigger than life to me.

My dad wanted to get a picture, so John Denver put his arm around me, and we smiled for the camera. With the first shot, the flash didn't go off, so there was some discussion of whether the picture had "taken" or not.

"Well, Dad, you better take another one," said John Denver. The whole thing was a surreal experience for an 11-year-old and I felt like I was on a cloud when I left there that night.

The next day, it was fun sharing my experience at school. Everyone wanted to hear about my "brush with greatness," and I gained even more notoriety because of it.

In the spring of my sixth grade year, students were excited to learn there would be a school talent show. A couple of seventh grade girls asked me about entering with them, and playing and singing, too. We were going to do Linda Ronstadt's "When Will I Be Loved?" Somebody else encouraged me to enter on my own too because you could enter with a group and then also as a solo act. I decided I would do that because I loved any opportunity to play. The day of the show came, and both songs went well. I felt like the girls and I did a good job, and my song seemed to be a hit as well. I sang one of my favorite "gimmick" songs of the day called "Junk Food Junkie." It was a song about a guy who was supposed to be a health food nut, and he would keep up the act by day; but by night he was a "junk food junkie," eating Twinkies, moon pies, and everything bad. The song always got a lot of laughs, and I had a couple of those gimmick songs in my bag at that point. I thought the middle school audience would like this song better; even then I was learning to "read" my audience and know what they'd respond to. I honestly never gave it a thought as to who would win; I just enjoyed the experience of playing.

There was a first, second, and third place, and I was surprised when they called the names of the group I was in as the second place winners. The girls were so excited, and they grabbed me by the arms, and we went out on stage to accept our award. We went and sat back down, still reveling in the moment and not even thinking about the first prize. I was totally shocked when they called my name as the first-place winner! The girls immediately sprang into action, knowing I would need some assistance to get back out front. They were my buddies from church too, so they knew me well, and it was like they were excited for me and wanted to share in that moment too. My parents were there for support too, just like they'd always been, for every win and every heartbreak as well. I spent the rest of the day going around to different classes in the school, singing a few songs for each, again allowing the music to break down barriers for me and take me places I never could have gone without it.

The summer after my sixth grade year was carefree, and I was glad to have a break from the pressure of the academic aspect of school. The days were hot and unusually dry that summer. Long days were spent with neighborhood friends, thinking up creative ways to pass the time. Sometimes the creative things were a little too creative and got us into serious trouble. One of those times was when my friends Rusty, Brian, and I decided it would be fun to destroy some of our old Hot Wheels cars. We determined that clearly the best way to do this would be to blow them up with some M80s in the woods where we normally played. We carefully set the stage for the apocalyptic event, placing the M80 fireworks underneath the cars. We had some matches and tried to light the M80s, but they wouldn't catch despite our best efforts. I knew where an old Zippo lighter was of my dad's, so I stealthily crept through the house to the old box in the basement where I knew I would find the lighter. Sure enough, it was there, so I slipped it in my pocket and headed back to the woods.

The lighter accomplished what the matches would not, and following the explosion of the M80s, the little Hot Wheels were soon ablaze. Unfortunately, though, the fire had spread to a pile of brush that we typically played in and referred to as our "fort." We were trying to figure out how to put out the fire, but it just kept spreading. The woods were behind Brian's house, and Brian's grandmother was staying with Brian and his little sister while his parents were out of town on a business trip. She looked out the window and saw smoke coming up from the trees. She was alarmed and immediately called the fire department. The fire station was literally around the corner, and the fire was put out in short order. It was a stupid stunt that could have had a really bad ending. I suppose in today's times, we might have been sent to juvenile court or something similar. While nothing like that happened, we did suffer the consequences with our parents, and I was grounded from playing with Rusty and Brian for the rest of the summer.

With summer vacation drawing to a close, I was looking forward to starting back to school and seeing all my friends again. I would be going to a new school, Gainesville Middle School, because the school system was making some changes, and middle school would now be grades 7 and 8 instead of 6 and 7 as it had been at Fair Street Middle School. The building was nice and new, and it was a very pleasant place.

One of the classes I was taking was a Music Appreciation/ Introduction to Songwriting class taught by Charles Mann. Charles was an "artist in residence" at Gainesville Middle School and was able to be at our school and teach for a time through a grant program. Students who had a particular interest in music were handpicked to participate in the class. We learned about different styles of music, how to write a song, and the structure of songwriting. He taught us a lot about music in general, and we got the chance to try our own hand at songwriting. I usually brought my guitar to class since it came in handy for writing; and one day when I came in, Mr. Mann asked me to sing for the class. That particular day, he had set up a sound system in the band room and brought a reel-to-reel tape machine. He taped me as I sang and played for nearly an hour for the class. I didn't know it at the time, but he was compiling information about me to be used later in a project he was involved in.

We found out just before Christmas that Mr. Mann was to be on a show that aired on WSB TV channel 2 called Sound of Youth, which featured young people in Georgia who excelled in various activities. To my surprise, he asked me if I wanted to be on the show with him and sing a couple of songs. I was very excited and of course said yes! We went to WSB on a Sunday in January for the taping, and I really enjoyed the whole process. I sang two songs, "Handy Man" by James Taylor, which I sang a lot during that time, and "Summer" by John Denver. The show aired the following Sunday on WBS and then the next week on the local PBS station. Once again, the exposure from this experience meant I was becoming even more well known in my school and hometown.

This happy time was marred, though, by the sudden illness in the fall of the year of my mother's father, whom I called Papa Rail. Papa was diagnosed with cancer, and we watched him quickly decline over a seven-week period. He died two days after Christmas. It was very difficult for me because I had a special relationship with Papa Rail, and he was the first person that I was close to who had died. It was painful to watch Nanny and my mother too while they grieved. But with the new year and then spring, I would feel the same hopeful feeling I'd felt in previous years, despite the great loss.

In the spring, I again found myself in the talent show, reveling in any opportunity to sing for my classmates. I sang "Lay Down Sally" by Eric Clapton, a popular song on the charts at that time. I won first place again that year, and they wanted me to come out and do an encore. I sang "Hot Legs" by Rod Stewart, and the kids went crazy! They loved it, but I think some of the teachers didn't quite know how to take it. The next year, I was barred from entering the talent show since I had won two years in a row. They told me I had an "unfair advantage" and that I could enter as a part of a group, but not as a solo act. It really made me mad at first because I thought that decision was unfair, but I played for another group that sang and tried to be a good sport and make the best of it.

It was in my eighth-grade year that we began to visit First Baptist Church of Gainesville. The pastor at our home church had left to serve elsewhere, and my parents sensed that it was time for our family to make a change as well. I remember feeling very much at home at the First Baptist Church of Gainesville, and after several weeks of visiting, our family made the decision to join. Following the service the morning we joined, we were in the "receiving line" where we were greeted by members welcoming us into the fellowship. One of those who came through the line was Steve Brown, youth minister at FBC. He greeted me and said he hoped I'd start coming to youth activities. Just behind him was an older lady who shook my hand and said, "Oh, you're just going to love him. He is so crazy! He showed up to a youth event in a 'shaving cream shirt' the other night. Took his shirt off and was completely covered in shaving cream!"

I thought, *Wow, that does sound crazy.*

Not long after, I did start to attend youth activities. Our Wednesday night program was called AWOL (A way of Life), and I was welcomed and immediately felt a part of the group. Steve had an Ovation guitar and asked me to play one night before the youth service started. I played for about twenty minutes, singing the top 40 songs that I knew and was accustomed to playing. After the service, he asked me to play some more, so I played again for about twenty minutes, and the kids who could stay gathered around.

Contemporary Christian music was in its infancy, and I didn't know many of the popular Christian songs of the day. Steve always allowed me to play the songs I knew and didn't judge me because I wasn't singing "Christian" music. As I look back now, I know he was seizing the opportunity to mentor me, which he would do throughout my teenage years. It wasn't long before Steve started asking me to go with him and sing at places where he was asked to speak. The first place he asked me to go and do a program was the Juvenile Detention Center in Gainesville. He went there once a month and spent the afternoon trying to connect and mentor the teenagers who had already made some bad decisions which had landed them in that place. Steve brought his guitar and a sound system the day I went with him. I played almost the whole afternoon in the cafeteria where the group met. Again I was singing the songs I knew, and they all seemed to love it and really responded well. I remember they kept scooting their chairs closer, and nobody wanted to leave when it was time to go. I saw the power the music had to help me connect with these teens whose backgrounds were likely very different from my own. During this period, Steve was helping me think about the "spiritual" side of my music and the impact it could have on people—while still being the crazy, fun-loving person that endeared him to all of us.

In February of that year, Steve asked me to go sing at a Valentine banquet he'd been asked to speak at in a town just north of us. Steve, my dad, and I made the thirty-mile trip to Clarkesville Baptist Church for the banquet, and we had some great conversation along the way. Steve was always very interested in what was going on with me and my music. On the way home, he said, "I can't wait for you to meet a friend of mine from Louisiana. He's coming to do the music for our revival services at the church." A few months later, I would meet Byron Cutrer, and I thought his talent was nothing short of incredible. Byron, a dyed-in-the-wool Cajun from New Orleans, and Steve had attended Mississippi College together and had become the best of friends. Steve had told Byron about me, and Byron wanted to hear me play and sing. I played for him one night following the revival service, and he was very encouraging to me.

"Brotha, that was awesome," he said in his pronounced Cajun accent.

He wanted to know if I played the piano, and I said I played a little but admitted that I wasn't very good at it. "If I could play like you, though, I'd play all the time," I told him. I never dreamed just what a pivotal role he would play in my life in such a short time.

Steve was always looking for opportunities to connect and meet us where we were in our young lives. One night in April of 1979, I picked up the phone, and Steve was on the line.

"What are you doing?" he asked.

"Homework." I said.

"Finish it, because I'm sending Cheryl [his wife] over to pick you up. I've got some people coming over, and we're going to start an ensemble," he said matter-of-factly.

At Steve's house, I went down in the basement, and a group had already started to gather there. Steve had a reel-to-reel machine with the accompaniment tracks we would use to sing with, which at that time had to be purchased from the record company. The first song we did was titled "Give Them All to Jesus."

> *Verse 1*
> Are you tired of chasing pretty rainbows
> Are you tired of spinning round and round
> Wrap up all the shattered dreams of your life
> And at the feet of Jesus lay them down

Chorus
Give them all
Give them all
Give them all to Jesus
Shattered dreams
Wounded hearts
Broken toys
Give them all
Give them all
Give them all to Jesus
And He will turn your sorrow into joy

Verse 2
He never said you'd only see sunshine
He never said there'd be no rain
He only promised a heart full of singing
About the very things that once caused pain

I suppose those lyrics pretty much summed up my life to that point, and through the music being introduced to me, I started to connect more with songs that had Christian messages.

Another significant song in our repertoire was "Rise Again," which Dallas Holm, a well-known Christian singer at that time, made popular.

When we were practicing, Steve said, "All right, Dowdy, I want you to jump out there and sing the verses. And, group, you're going to back him up on the choruses."

After we'd practiced and had enough songs to do a program, the first place we sang in public was at Lakeshore Mall in Gainesville. We had a sound system, and I remember stepping out from the group to sing the verses on "Rise Again." It was a different experience, singing with an accompaniment track and hearing all the instrumentation and the rest of the group behind me, not just a guitar like I was accustomed to. I also felt that there was a difference when I sang these songs that I couldn't quite explain. I felt the power in the lyrics, and I knew somehow that I was singing about things that were important, and it made me feel good to be a part of that, even as a thirteen-year-old boy. My own faith was growing and being strengthened as I watched Steve and others live out their faith in front of me week by week.

Later that summer, I would have my second experience with Byron Cutrer as he came to do the music for the summer camp we had in Panama City, Florida. Byron could play various instruments, and he brought his drum set that week. In the evening services, he would play drum solos for us.

I remember thinking, *This guy's a minister of music, and he can do all that!*

I was amazed by his talent and wanted to learn more from him. Little did I know at the time, I would soon have the chance.

Chapter 7

Bull's-Eye and Bravado

In my eighth grade year, I became involved in the Boy Scouts, which would have a huge impact on my life. First Baptist Church had a rich tradition of sponsoring Troop 26, which met on the church campus. I was first introduced to the idea of joining Scouts through a friend of mine, Tim Black. One night at an after-church fellowship, he came and sat down beside me.

"Why don't you join Scouts?" he asked. "I could be your helper and get credit toward my Eagle Scout."

I thought it over for a few days and decided to give it a try. So that was how it worked. Tim was my mentor, showing me the ropes and giving any special assistance I required during our activities. Scout meetings were once a week on Monday nights from seven to nine. When I started going in November, I didn't even have a uniform and had to borrow gear from my cousins for my first camping trip in December. They loaned me a sleeping bag, backpack, and a six-inch sheath knife, which I learned later was contraband. I turned it in to the Scoutmaster but was able to get it back at the end of the trip.

Our first camping trip was spending the weekend on a local farm, just to get our feet wet before we tried more challenging terrain. When I say "get our feet wet," though, that was an understatement. In fact, whole bodies were soaked to the skin when, on Sunday morning, we woke up to our tents and sleeping bags full of water from a steady rain that had come down as we slept. To make matters worse, the night before, some of the boys had started eating cinnamon by the spoonsful, just to see how much they could tolerate. I felt like I'd eaten my weight in cinnamon, and that morning when I woke up, I was as sick as I could be, throwing up every few minutes until there was nothing more left. I did survive that camping trip, the first of many such experiences.

That Christmas, I received all the gear I would need for future camping trips: North Face sleeping bag, backpack, waterproof boots, and jacket. I think my dad had enjoyed going to the local sporting goods store and telling them, "Just outfit him with whatever he needs." I got my actual Scout badge in January and started earning merit badges shortly thereafter. Tim helped me all the way through, especially where there was writing involved, which there was quite a bit of on the quizzes for merit badges. Right away, I decided that if I was going to do this, I wanted to make a mark. I knew almost immediately I wanted to go for Eagle Scout. I started racking up merit badges, even earning leadership skill awards, putting me in position to later be on leadership corps.

I learned a great deal about responsibility in Scouts and about giving back to the community. One of our community responsibilities was overseeing a semitrailer on the church property where people came to toss their old newspapers. This was our own form of recycling before it was popular. Each Patrol had "paper truck duty" for one month following our meetings, and then each patrol would spend one Saturday each year organizing and stacking the materials on the truck. On camping trips, everybody had a responsibility too. Mine was usually to set up the dining fly along with one other Scout. We had to go get the chuck box and large stand off the truck and set it up in the tent. Then there was a big water tank that had to be filled up, and we were responsible for filling it the first time. Aside from helping to set up the camp, our own tents were inspected once we had our gear off the truck and into place. It was like a small military operation—our uniforms being inspected on a regular basis also.

Even though I liked these camping trips, I was always ready to get home, and while I enjoyed the camaraderie with the boys, I wanted to move through getting the merit badges as quickly as I could. One of the badges, which was an extreme highlight to me, was the aviation merit badge. For six weeks, the seven boys who'd signed up to work on the badge met on another night besides our regular meeting night. Tim's father, Reuben Black, was a pilot for Delta and was responsible for teaching us what we needed to know to be checked off for the aviation badge. We learned about aerodynamics, different types of airplanes, and what it took to actually make something fly and keep it in the air. We learned the "aeronautic alphabet" and how to do a checklist for takeoff. We also had to build a model plane of some kind and prepare a very thorough report about the airplane we built. We could have help building the model, so my dad helped me, doing the detail work that was more difficult for me. The airplane I chose was the L-1011, the same kind of plane I was on that shot suddenly into the sky to avoid landing on top of another plane. I still remember some of the specifications of that plane from the report, like the fact that it stood fifty-seven feet off the ground and had eleven-foot windows.

The end of the six-week period culminated with Reuben taking us up in a Cessna 172, a four-seater. He let each of us take our turn at "flying" the plane from the right seat, giving each boy control of the yoke when it was his turn. Reuben taught us how to do turns and pull back on the yoke to go up and push forward to go down. It was an experience I'll never forget. I just remember feeling excitement, no fear or hesitation, when it was my turn to sit in the copilot seat. I had a mild interest in aviation before that, but being in the plane with the controls in my hands really gave me a passion for flying. I knew that if I had been able, I would have started studying right then to be a pilot.

Another highlight of the scouting year was summer camp, a time to focus in on earning merit badges, especially those that had to be done outside. We'd go to Camp Rainy Mountain, the mecca for Boy Scouts in North Georgia for a week every summer. Things were a little cushier than our typical camping trips because the tents were built on wooden foundations, and we actually had cots to sleep on. There were two people to a tent, which had a little more room than our regular tents, and there were inspections of the tents and our uniforms every morning. Our day started at 7:30 a.m. with breakfast, and we were working on merit badges by 8:00 a.m. That first year, I got all of my aquatic merit badges out of the way: swimming, lifesaving, and rowing. I had been a good swimmer for several years, having spent many hours at the Elk's Club pool, becoming comfortable in the water. For the swimming merit badge, we had to swim one mile across the lake in four minutes. I remember being so tired when I finished, but I made it the first time I tried. Lifesaving was the most difficult: we had to see how long we could tread water with our clothes on. We then had to take our clothes off, down to our shorts, and make a floatation device with them, all the while treading water. The most unnerving activity by far, though, was when we had to dive fourteen feet to retrieve a cinder block from the bottom of the lake.

Tim and I swam out to the area of the cinder block.

"Okay, you're right over it," he said. "Just dive straight down and feel around for it."

I got a good breath and headed down to the bottom, feeling a little anxious, but not wanting to show it. I went down at an angle and had to search a few seconds but found it fairly quickly. I pulled it out of the silt bottom of the lake and headed up to the surface. The block was light in the water, but once I reached the surface, it began to get heavy as I swam with it back to the dock. I was still a fairly small fellow at age thirteen, not yet having gone through my teenage growth spurt. I probably weighed one hundred pounds soaking wet, and I bet that block weighed twenty. Relief flooded over me as I reached my destination and handed off the cinder block to waiting hands at the dock.

In the spring of my first year in Scouts, I had earned the rank to enable me to assume an office, and so I became troop musician. I was responsible for the music for our "church service" on Sunday morning during camping trips, picking out the hymns and songs, memorizing them, and then leading the group. I also played for other special events as needed and just for fun around the campfire as well. Even in this setting, music helped me find my place among my peers during those sometimes-awkward teenage years.

As I began my ninth grade year of school, I had all the apprehensions that high school freshmen typically do, with the added worry of having to learn a brand-new building I had not been in before. I was not to have any special assistance getting to and from classes, so making sure I knew my way around was a big concern for me. A few days before school started, my resource counselor, Lynn Bryant, gave me a very detailed tour of the school and showed me where everything was that I would possibly need. I had my schedule in braille, and we spent a couple of hours walking the halls, to familiarize me with the layout. There was no braille on the room numbers back then, so I had to learn the rooms and know where I was going from that point on. The school was arranged in a sort of *E* formation, with a long hall and three halls coming off it. Then the three halls had annexes where the fine arts, gym, and vocational areas were. We also had a Christian education building, and we had to go outside and down "elephant trail" for some distance to get to it. So there was a lot of movement throughout the day, and it was very crowded, the largest crowds I had ever been in, which was nerve-wracking. After the first couple of days, though, I settled in and started to feel more comfortable in my surroundings.

One place I immediately felt comfortable was Chorus. It was the first year of teaching at Gainesville High School for Wendell Carpenter, whom I was already familiar with as one of our musicians at First Baptist Church. There were older students in Chorus who seemed to take me under their wing right away and made me feel a part of the group. We sang some great music that year, and one of those songs was "Yesterday" by the Beatles. We had tryouts for the solo part on the song, and I decided to give it a try, even though I didn't think I stood much of a chance as a freshman. Dr. Carpenter played for me to sing, and he had some positive things to say to me, but I was still surprised when he announced that I was going to sing the solo. My peers told me that was very unusual because the previous director would never give freshmen that opportunity. We sang so many places that year, including the Capitol in Washington, DC, and I sang "Yesterday" all year long. We were supposed to sing at the White House also, but the morning we got there was when the failed attempt to rescue the American hostages from Iran had taken place, and the White House was closed to all visitors.

Chorus gave me a place to belong at school, and I had plenty of friends, but academically I was struggling more than ever. I had Algebra II at that point, and as we got into higher-order math, it was difficult to do everything in braille. English was a struggle too, and sometimes in other subjects I didn't pay attention like I should have, and some assignments I blew off entirely. I always enjoyed history and was normally well prepared for that class. One day, however, I had not studied for a vocabulary-spelling quiz I knew I had to pass. In history class, I had a special desk that was made to accommodate the braille typewriter and related supplies. It had a small alcove underneath the work surface where paper and supplies could be stored. It was the one and only time I ever tried to cheat on a test, but I had a list of the spelling words in the alcove. I tried to casually rest my hand in the alcove so I could double-check myself before I started to type the answers as the teacher called out the words. We were about halfway through the test, and I really thought everything was going fine until my teacher started walking toward the back of the class. She walked straight to my desk and reached her hand in the alcove, discovering the paper with the answers.

"I'll take that," she said. "You can finish the rest of the test, but this grade will be a zero!"

I felt so humiliated, lower than dirt at that moment, and it was enough to cure me of ever trying anything like that again. While I was barely keeping my head above water academically, socially, life was pretty good. My sister had just learned to drive, and she and I could go places, which gave both of us a bit more freedom.

While we did our share of "fighting" like siblings do, I loved it when she'd say, "Do you want to go for a ride?"

We'd ride around Gainesville, enjoying our newfound independence. Church continued to be an important part of my life, giving me another place where I felt I belonged. One Wednesday night, we got word that AWOL would meet in the Scout Cabin. Troop 26 had a very nice cabin on the grounds of the church, and we walked into the cabin that December night to a warm, roaring fire in the fireplace. In the middle of a group of adults at the front of the cabin stood Byron Cutrer. We were totally shocked because none of us kids knew he was going to be there. We didn't know what was going on but would soon hear an important announcement from Steve Brown. Steve had recently become senior pastor of First Baptist after the previous Pastor retired, leaving the youth group in the capable hands of some dedicated volunteers for a short time. Steve got up to talk, and the room immediately fell quiet.

"We've got an announcement to make. Byron's coming to be our music guy, and he's also going to take over youth since they've given me this other responsibility."

Everybody was so excited, and they stood up and cheered. We all loved Byron, even then, with the limited experiences we'd had with him to that point. Byron and his family moved to Gainesville from Louisiana by January, and he started making big plans for us as soon as he arrived. Byron called a choir rehearsal the first week he was here, and what was normally a small number turned into a large group that day. I had been a part of the ensemble but had never been a part of the larger group. Byron announced that we would do a musical in March of that year. He said we were going to rent Pearce Auditorium at Brenau College for three nights of performances of *Celebrate Life*, a big youth musical at that time. Byron took me aside later and asked if I'd rather sing or play guitar as part of the rhythm section in the musical. I said I'd rather play the guitar, and I was excited about playing with the other musicians. Byron went out and recruited other players because we'd never had other instruments besides piano and organ at First Baptist.

In less than three months, we put that musical on to a packed house all three nights. I spent a good bit of time with Byron learning the parts for the musical, and I soon learned that he was a serious musician. He could cut you to the quick with a remark, but you knew he was right, and then you loved him again in five minutes' time. The guitar parts were difficult, but he pushed me and made me a better musician as I worked through it. After the musical, he told us we were going on choir tour. I again played guitar, enjoying honing my skills as I mastered some harder material. We went to New Orleans and through Mississippi, areas Byron knew well, singing and playing, some sixty kids and several adult chaperones. When we got home from choir tour, Byron had a couple of summer camps he had committed to do music for. He asked me to go with him.

"Grab your guitar, and we'll sing and play some stuff together," he said.

I did two camps with him that summer, and he even paid me to go. I would have done it just to get to play and to hang out with Byron, but he insisted on paying me. Those were formative times for me, both musically and spiritually, helping me grow, belong, and enjoy the life God had given me.

I continued to progress in Scouts during that year, earning merit badges, going on the monthly scouting trips, and attending weekly meetings. Part of our time was spent fund-raising for a high adventure trip we were to take in the summer, a trip that would span several states. We had a "chicken Q" where we smoked chickens over a pit and sold them to the community. Another big fund-raising event was the Scout show, where we had different exhibits showcasing our work during the year, and I sold one hundred tickets, which paid for my trip and then some.

A regional event called the *camporee* was held twice a year so that all the troops of the Northeast Georgia Council could have some interaction with one another, and it was also a time that parents could come and see what the Scouts were doing. It was held at "Scoutland," which was a large open camping area adjacent to the lake just past the Chattahoochee Country Club in Gainesville. The various troops would have competitions during these events: who could tie the fastest knot, who could build the most efficient fire, and so on. Saturday nights were the big family night, and there were easily one thousand people there, with parents and Scouts. We had a big campfire, and various skits were presented during the evening. I had sung for two of these events before, once in the eighth grade and once in the ninth. This was the second camporee of the year, and I was to again provide the music that Saturday night.

In the morning at breakfast, one of my buddies asked me, "What are you going to sing tonight?"

"I don't really know," I said.

At that point, I had quite a few songs in my repertoire, and I felt comfortable singing any one of them.

Another boy piped up, "You ought to sing 'My Ding-a-Ling!'"

"I don't know," I said. "I've never sung it before."

"You do know it, though, don't you?" asked Robert Shire, a boy who was always one to push the envelope a bit.

"I think so," I said, and I went to get my guitar.

I started playing and singing the Chuck Berry song that my buddies knew so well. The more I sang, the harder they laughed, and pretty soon some of them were rolling around on the ground, barely able to breathe.

"You have to do it tonight," one of them said.

"Do it! Do it!" they all began to chant.

"I *dare* you to do it!" said Joel Broxton, a fun-loving, enthusiastic boy.

Daring me to do something was a surefire way to get me to fully commit because I was always going to take a dare. At that point, the deal was all but sealed, any second thoughts pushed aside. We went about our day, doing all the things that were required of us. Night came, and it was time for the bonfire, time for my homage to "My Ding-a-ling." I gave what I thought at the time was a masterful introduction.

"I want to sing a little song that had a special meaning to me and my patrol mates this morning. I've never done this song before, so let's see how it goes."

I launched right into the clever lyrics with the blatant double entendre:

> When I was a little bitty boy
> My grandma bought me a cute little toy
> Two silver bells on a string
> She told me it was my ding-a-ling-a-ling
>
> My ding-a-ling, my ding-a-ling, won't you play with my
> ding-a-ling-a-ling
> My ding-a-ling, my ding-a-ling, won't you play with my
> ding-a-ling-a-ling

By the fourth verse, I was hitting my stride. The boys were sing-ing along full voice, and I continued:

> Once while swimming across turtle creek
> Man, them snappers right at my feet
> Sure was hard swimming cross that thing
> With both hands holding my ding-a-ling

I finished with the final scandalous verse:

> Now this here song ain't too bad
> Prettiest song you ever had
> And those of you who will not sing
> Must be playing with your own ding-a-ling

Then the boys joined me on the final chorus when I sang, "My," and pointed at them, and they sang, "Ding-a-ling." Others joined in, and we finished out the chorus that way.

People were clapping, laughing, doing a little bit of everything, but I knew the minute I finished, I was in deep trouble.

"Thank you and good night," I said.

My mother was especially mortified, verbally berating me with, "I can't believe that you would do something like that and embarrass us!"

My dad was a little calmer. "Well, I guess you'll get what's com-ing to you at the meeting Monday night."

I did, in fact, get what was coming to me when I got called into the scoutmaster's office Monday night. I was given a lecture about "poor judgment" and told that if I ever pulled any shenanigans like that again, I would be relieved of my duties as troop musician. I kept to the straight and narrow after that. I was looking forward to the high adventure trip in June and didn't want to do anything to jeopardize that.

We left on a Wednesday shortly after school was out on a char-tered Greyhound bus and made the long trip to Fort Campbell, Kentucky. We arrived at the Fort Campbell Army Base late Wednesday afternoon. That evening, we saw a movie, *The Buddy Holly Story*, at the movie theater on the base. We spent the night in the barracks and the next morning were taken on a tour of the base. We saw the men in training and were able to look at different helicopters and vehicles up close. Following the tour of the base, we made the hour trip to Nashville, Tennessee, where we visited Belmont College, which had a cutting-edge music program. It was a pivotal day for me because it was the first time I ever went into a recording studio, and it was worth the whole trip to me just to do that.

We went from there to see Charlie Daniels's ranch that was being built just outside Nashville. Our scoutmaster had a connection to Charlie Daniels and was somehow able to arrange the tour. We even got to go through the house that was under construction at the time. We went from there to the Grand Ole Opry, and I got to stand on the circle in the center of the stage, which is a thrill for any young budding musician. We finished up the day at the Opryland amusement park and then headed back to spend another night at the army base. We boarded the bus the next morning and headed for Arkansas, making a pit stop in Memphis to see Graceland on the way.

We arrived at the Buffalo River in Arkansas late Friday and made camp for the night. We were in the water in canoes and rafts the next morning by nine o'clock. I was in a canoe with one of the leaders, and we worked in tandem to negotiate the rapids, which were just rough enough to be fun. We stayed in the water until about two thirty and, later in the day, went to explore some underground caverns led by a tour guide. Sunday, we broke camp and headed for Vicksburg, Mississippi, to hike the Vicksburg Trail. The trail was fourteen miles long, and it took us about seven hours with a few stops along the way to hike the entire length of the trail.

It was very hot in Mississippi in June, and canteens had to be filled several times along the way. Following the hike, the troop headed back to camp—hot, tired, and sweaty. The adults then announced that we had done a little better with expenses on the trip and would be able to stay in a Holiday Inn in Jackson that last night. We were all so excited just to be able to shower and sleep in a real bed after a week of roughing it.

Scouting activities filled the summer, culminating with camp at Rainy Mountain, where it was again time to make significant progress toward earning merit badges. One morning in the line for breakfast, our scoutmaster asked me if I wanted to try for my marksmanship merit badge.

I had no idea how that would be possible, but I said, "Sure, but how would I do that?"

Evidently, he had been thinking about it because he asked the marksmanship instructor standing next to us, "Do you think we could rig a cowbell up over the target and attach a rope to it so we could ring the bell from the shooter's platform? Then he could shoot in the direction of the sound."

The instructor was in favor of giving it a try, although I think everyone was skeptical that I could achieve consistent results. Immediately, the plan was set in motion; and by that afternoon, I was on my stomach on the shooter's platform, rifle in my hands. I had fired a BB gun in the past, but had never shot with anything more powerful than that, so I was looking forward to shooting the rifle, even if the plan failed as far as being able to hit the target with accuracy. The instructor showed me the basics of the firearm and then centered me up with the target, which was too far away for me to see at all. The first time I fired, I was surprised at the power of the rifle because it did kick back quite a bit. I aimed for the sound of the bell, and the bullet hit the target, but nowhere near the bull's-eye the first time. The next time I fired, I was more ready for the kick back and held the rifle steady, getting closer to the bull's-eye with the second shot. I practiced for about an hour, feeling more comfortable and steadier with every shot, hitting the cardboard target with increasing accuracy. I had hit all around the target, but hitting the actual bull's-eye eluded me.

"See if you can hit the bull's-eye now," the instructor encouraged.

The bell rang, and I did my best to zero in on the sound. I steadied the rifle and took my best shot. A split second later, I heard a powerful *ping* of lead striking metal. Unbelievably to most of my peers, instructors, and even to myself, I had shot a hole straight through that bell! There was a great deal of excitement and disbelief that I had hit the bell, but I still wanted to hit the actual bull's-eye, which was a couple of feet below the bell. I again steadied myself and took aim at what I thought was the area a little below the sound. This time, I hit it, square in the center, to the whoops and hollers of everyone present. They gave me the cowbell and the target as a memento of the accomplishment, and probably as proof I would be able to show to anyone who didn't believe the story!

Summer came to a close, and I was disappointed but not surprised to learn that I had not passed a couple of my core classes, English and science, and would not be considered a tenth grader in the upcoming school year. I would have to repeat my ninth grade English and science, but I would be in tenth grade classes for all other courses. I would, however, be in a ninth grade homeroom, which humiliated me terribly. After about three weeks of school in my freshman homeroom, it was beginning to sink in that I would have to be in school an additional year, wouldn't graduate with my class, and would be with the group that had been behind me at least part of the time from now on. I thought it over and decided to propose an idea to Curtis Seagers, our principal. Mr. Seagers had a gruff exterior but really cared about the students. He was perfect for the job, almost having a military-style approach, even looking the part with his flat-top haircut. I saw him in the hall one Monday morning.

"Could I talk to you?" I asked.

"Sure, come on in my office," he said.

I began nervously, "I know I messed up last year, and I know I'm where I deserve to be, but I just don't want to be here another year. I mean, I like y'all and everything, but I just don't want to spend five years in high school."

"Well, Dowdy, what choice do you have?" asked Mr. Segars.

"I've got a deal for you," I continued boldly.

"I'm listenin'," he barked.

"Well, I'm taking more tenth grade classes than ninth. If I make all As this semester, would you consider promoting me to a tenth grade homeroom and consider me a tenth grader?" I asked.

"Well, now, this is not the kind of decision I can just make by myself," Mr. Segars reasoned.

"Well, who else do we need to talk to?" I pressed on.

"We should talk to Mr. Nelson, and I'll call him right now," said Mr. Segars.

Mr. Nelson, our counselor, came to the office, and Mr. Segars announced, "This young man has an ambitious proposal for us."

I shared my plan with Mr. Nelson, and after some discussion, Mr. Segars said, "This might be a possibility. We'll have to discuss it some more, and we'll let you know by Friday."

I thanked them and went on my way, wondering all week if my proposal stood a prayer of being accepted, or if I could even pull off all As since I'd never made all As so far in my school career. Friday came, and walking down the hall, I heard Mr. Segars call out to me. He had the habit of just yelling things at people in the hall, not in a mean way but in his military style.

"Dowdy, if you're going to make the cut, you'd better pull up your grades," he barked.

"Is that a yes?" I yelled back.

"Make all As," was his reply.

I was really excited and vowed to myself that I was going to buckle down like never before.

As it turned out, from a social aspect, things weren't that different for me even with my demoted status. In fact, I started meeting and then hanging out with some upperclassmen as the year progressed. One of those seniors was Jeff Miller, stepson of Sonny Allegro, who first asked me to sing at his restaurant back when I was ten years old. Jeff was going to audition for a role in a production at Gainesville College and asked if I would play piano to accompany him. I had never played piano in public before at that point. I had been teaching myself, practicing at home for about a year, having been inspired by Byron Cutrer to get better at it, but still wasn't very secure in my playing. I was fifteen years old, going to play for a college audition, which was rather intimidating. Ed Cabell, the director of drama at Gainesville College, heard me play that day and asked me what grade I was in.

"So how many more years till you get here? We sure could use you in the drama department and music department too," said Mr. Cabell.

I was encouraged by those words and also by other opportunities that came out of the audition. A couple of girls from Gainesville High School also auditioned that day and apparently told some of their friends about my playing. The Miss GHS pageant was coming up, and I started receiving phone calls from girls to play the piano to accompany them in the pageant. I played for no less than seven girls in the pageant that year, which I thought was a really good gig as a fifteen-year-old boy. One of the girls I played for was crowned Miss GHS, but I enjoyed practicing with every one of them.

Another opportunity I had starting in tenth grade was playing for the pregame meal before the football games. They asked me to come and play and sing for about half an hour before every home game. I also had people who weren't with the football program who would come just to hear the music. One day, Pam Ware, drama director, came up to me after I finished.

"Honey, you are just toooo good," she said with her dramatic flair. "You need to be in drama. We're doing *Grease* next semester, and you need to be in it!"

"I don't act," I said.

"You can at least play in the band, but you need to be in drama, so come and see me and get signed up for next semester."

I thought it sounded like fun, so I took Mrs. Ware up on her offer and signed up for drama for the following semester.

As the first semester of the year progressed, I really applied myself to my studies in a way I had not done before, and I was maintaining an A average in every class. Mr. Nelson would question me every week or two.

"How is it going?" he'd ask with concern.

"All As," I'd say.

"Okay, I'm checking," he'd reply.

The semester came to a close, and we got our schedules for the next semester. My schedule was printed for me in braille, and there, at the top, was my homeroom assignment, "10 J." I had made it! They also put me up in a tenth grade science and English class so I would be able to graduate on time. I had learned my lesson, and even though I was never a star student, I never let myself get in the position of failing any subject again.

Just before the first semester ended, I joined my first band, at the request of an older friend of mine, Chris Fight, who was in chorus with me. Chris came and sat down behind me in a school assembly one day.

"There are these guys that want to start a band. I told them I'd bring you to rehearsal next Thursday night," he said excitedly.

Chris had gotten a key from Dr. Carpenter to the chorus room, which could be entered from outside the building, and our group met there. There were four of us guys and a girl singer, Sandy Waters. I was the youngest player, and I played rhythm guitar and keyboards. We had a drummer, bass player, and lead guitar player. We thought it was so cool because the lead guitar player, Danny Benton, was a friend of one of the guys and was twenty-one, had a Porsche 911, and a Peavey Super Festival Amp. We played for a couple of hours that first night and immediately clicked. We began to put a playlist together: REO Speedwagon, Pat Benatar, Tom Petty and the Heartbreakers, among others. We started playing in public right away.

Pam Ware asked us to play for the dance at Thespian State Conference for two nights, and we played for various things at Gainesville High School. We practiced every week and played all through the spring, but it didn't last very long. Danny flaked out and went to the Cayman Islands, and we sort of broke up after that, but it had been a good experience for me, teaching me how to learn things quickly and "hang on" with musicians who were better than I was.

Chris continued to be an influence in my life even after the band broke up, although sometimes not for the better. While Chris was a good musician and a positive influence for me musically, he had a rebellious streak that had gotten him into trouble in the past, and I found myself wanting to fit in and follow his lead. There was a time when we cut third period nearly every day, going to the park across the street, playing guitars and singing Eagles' songs by the lake, even downing some beer from time to time that Chris had bought. I had accumulated seventeen absences in Pam Ware's speech class, and the jig was about to be up. We'd skip Mrs. Ware's class and then show up for drama in sixth period. Mrs. Ware let us know in no uncertain terms that it was very disrespectful to her to skip third period and then come waltzing in for drama in sixth period. Unbeknownst to me, Mr. Seagers called my parents to inquire about my absences. To my surprise, that night at supper, the question came from my dad.

"Where have you gone for seventeen days this semester?" he asked.

I was trying to think fast on my feet. "Nowhere. Why?" I asked nervously.

"Well, you haven't been in third period."

"How do you know that?" I asked.

"A little bird told me," he said.

We seemed to have a lot of little birds with information during my growing-up days.

"Well, when the weather started warming up, it was just too tempting not to be outside, so some of us went to play guitars over at the park," I explained, carefully leaving out the part about the beer.

I got a good talking-to and was too scared to cut class after that, not knowing how my parents had been informed of our little excursions and thinking twice about the second chance I'd been given that semester.

Chapter 8

Eagle Soars

While many things were happening in my tenth grade year, I was moving through the requirements to become an Eagle Scout as well. I had achieved the rank of Life Scout and was in the process of planning and executing my service project for Eagle. It took a while to get my project approved since it involved making changes to a federal building. My plan was to place braille and large-print signage in the federal building in Gainesville. There was no such signage in any of the buildings in Gainesville, even though it had been law that braille signs had to be placed in public buildings since 1969. I had to make phone calls to find out specific requirements and get permission to go ahead with the project.

One of those calls was to our Ninth District congressman, Ed Jenkins, who was instrumental in helping me get through the "red tape" of the process. Finally, the project was approved and the signs ordered by Frank Oliver, superintendent of the building. I rounded up the group of ten volunteers who would assist me that day. We placed some thirty signs in the federal building, mostly indicating stairwells and elevators, meeting the specific requirements that the signage had to be five feet high and so many inches from the doorjamb. An article titled "One Scout Aiming to Change the Dependence of the Blind" was written about the project by Robert Powell for our Gainesville newspaper, the *Times*.

In excerpts from that article, he writes,

> What others have not done for the blind in Hall County, a 15-year-old blind Boy Scout has done for himself. Mark Dowdy, a sophomore at

Gainesville High School, recently led an effort to have large print and Braille signs installed at the federal building downtown. The project will help satisfy community service requirements Mark must meet to become an Eagle Scout, the highest rank in scouting.

"I found out that none of the public buildings had any signs for the blind and thought what would I do if I had to go to any of them," Mark comments. "I think the signs will be a big help to handicapped people like myself."

[...] On December 5th, Mark led 10 volunteers in installing between 30 and 40 signs on stairs, elevators, exits, and restrooms in the building. Using a Braille tape measure, Mark measured the exact height, five feet, required for each sign, while helpers put the adhesive backed plastic signs in place. Mark had hoped to install signs identifying each agency in the building, but his plan was approved to meet only minimum federal requirements. Mark and his father, Bob Dowdy, would still like a directory in Braille installed in the building's entrance.

"I hope the city and county fathers pick up on this and do the other public buildings in town," Bob Dowdy says. He noted a federal law requiring signs for the blind in public buildings has been in effect since 1969.

[...]Before conducting this project, Mark had earned 21 merit badges on his way to becoming an Eagle Scout. His project will be reviewed by a committee. If approved, he will receive his Eagle insignia on Feb. 8.

Mark's scoutmaster, Fleming Weaver, appears to have no doubt the boy will be awarded the Eagle rank. "He has done an excellent job."

Weaver commented. "He has performed all the requirements any person would have to. There have been no concessions."

Weaver describes Mark as "an inspiration" to other members of his 63 member troop. "He is enthusiastic, a morale builder. His lack of sight has not handicapped him," the scoutmaster comments.

Mark, in fact, has led a very active scout life. Last summer he participated in a "high adventure" trip to several states, which included whitewater canoeing, hiking and exploring caves. Mark is also the troop musician, a title that hints at the talent that has led him to master the guitar, piano, organ and banjo.

[...] Despite his talents and his handicap, Mark most of all wants to be treated like everyone else. "People think because you're blind you need to be helped and they are sorry for you," he says. "but I really don't need help that much. If I need help, I always ask."

Mark believes that signs like those installed at the federal building will help blind people to become more independent. "It makes us less afraid of the outside world. Not having these things has kept us inhibited," he says.

Thanks to Mark's own efforts, maybe that will change.

So while the project was completed and I was waiting on the review from the committee for final approval, I had another challenge that would make getting around a little more difficult. Usually in January or February in our part of Georgia, we would have an ice storm, or at the very least, several days with icy roads. No fluffy snow, just dangerous "black ice" that was very unforgiving to tires or feet. One day in January, our band was headed into the chorus room at school to practice. I was walking backward down the icy steps carrying one end of a keyboard while Chris Fite had the other end. My foot slipped on the ice, and I twisted my ankle as I went down to the ground trying to protect the keyboard, which landed on top of my foot. I went ahead and practiced for several hours, even though my foot was hurting like crazy. I got home but didn't even mention it to my mom and dad because they were going somewhere that evening, and I didn't want to bother them with it. Later, though, when I tried to remove my shoe, my foot was so swollen the shoe wouldn't come off. With great effort, I finally pulled it off; and when my parents got home, my foot was black, blue, and swollen. They knew I had broken a bone and took me to the ER. Dr. Don Willers, an orthopedist, was called in to look at my foot.

"Son, you should have come to the office about four this afternoon. It would have been a lot easier than coming to the ER!"

My ankle was broken, and I had to be immobilized with my foot elevated for a couple of days while the plaster cast set up completely. I had a walking cast, so I was able to go back to school on Monday. I had the cast on for four weeks, a span of time during which several significant events occurred.

A few days after breaking my ankle, I learned that I had been selected to be the "Governor's Scout for a Day," a program Governor George Busbee had instituted in 1975. Georgia's Governor Busbee had been a Scout and wanted to do something for the scouting program in Georgia, so one Eagle Scout per month was selected to spend the day with the governor as essentially an honorary "staff member." A couple of weeks later, my dad and I headed down to the Capitol. We arrived, and the governor's assistant, Tom Purdue, met with us first and then ushered us in to meet Governor Busbee. He was very friendly and shook our hands, greeting us warmly.

My dad, assuming he would stay with us for the day as well, was surprised when Governor Busbee said, "Well, Mr. Dowdy, we'll see you back here at four thirty."

My dad, not knowing what to do with a whole day in Atlanta, finally decided to take a tour of the Lockheed-Martin facilities, where he stayed until time to come back and get me. After my dad left, Governor Busbee spent some time just talking to me about my scouting experiences and about music. I sat in on all his meetings that day in his office, some of which were really interesting; some of which were not.

All the while, though, I kept thinking, *I am in the governor's office!*

The morning went by quickly, and it was time to go to lunch. The governor wanted to go to his favorite restaurant in walking distance from the Capitol, a little burger place where he could go without a lot of fanfare. As far as my needs in getting around in unfamiliar places, I would typically just rely on touching the elbow of a person willing to lead me. Today the governor himself wanted to be that person, and we headed out to lunch with the governor's entourage, including Tom Perdue and the security detail, me at the governor's side, having the extra challenge of walking with the heavy cast on my leg. After we'd walked about a block, we met up with Maynard Jackson, mayor of Atlanta.

"Mayor, how are you today?" asked the governor.

"Fine, Governor," answered Mr. Jackson.

The governor introduced me to Mr. Jackson, and we shook hands.

"Whatcha up to today?" asked the governor in his South Georgia accent.

"City business, city business," replied the mayor.

"Why don'cha come on and have some lunch with us?" asked the governor.

So the mayor joined us also, and it was one of those moments where I again thought, *I can't believe this is happening to me!*

Now that I look back, I realize all the more the significance of the first blind Scout in Georgia having lunch with the first black mayor of Atlanta, both of us having broken new ground in our own way. I was honored to have been a part of the day, and that experience made it all the more special. An AP reporter named Dick Pettys wrote an article about my activities that day and sent to me the actual piece of paper signed by him with a note of encouragement, which came off the wire.

On February 8, he wrote for the *Atlanta AP*:

Want to know how the Governor spends his time when the Georgia Legislature is in session? A 15-year-old Boy Scout got a close-up view last week, and it's not the way you might think. There is, says Mark Dowdy of Gainesville, a lot of nitty-gritty talk about details of budgets, legislation, appointments and schedules when the door swings shut on the highest elected office in the state.

How does a Boy Scout rate sitting in on the rarefied atmosphere of the governor's office for top-level, shirt-sleeve discussions of state business?

Mark, an Eagle Scout, was just one of dozens of scouts who have earned that privilege through Gov. George Busbee's "Eagle Scout of the Month" program, which began when Busbee took office in 1975. Once a month, the various Boy Scout councils in Georgia send former Scout Busbee their top Eagle to serve on his staff for one day. Mark was unusual in just one respect: he has been legally blind since birth.

Nevertheless, he gets the highest marks from his Scoutmaster, Fleming Weaver, who says the boy has been "an inspiration" to the other boys in his troop.

What was his day with Busbee like? A series of meetings, mostly. "I got to hear the governor call a person and tell him he was going to be the new district attorney somewhere. Before that, the Governor and some other people had a list and they debated it and decided this person would be the best person for the job. So, he called him up and said, "Well, you're it. I'm going to swear you in next Tuesday at 10 o'clock."

Other meetings dealt with the budget and individual bills before the General Assembly, the Scout said.

"I had no idea he had to okay every little thing that came in there. If I had it to do, I don't know that I could do it," he added. Busbee's association Boy Scouts of America dates back to his own Scouting days when he was growing up in the Southwest Georgia town of Vienna. As an adult, Busbee also served as a merit badge counselor for the program's three citizenship badges.

After becoming Governor, Busbee explained, "I was looking for something that I could do for Scouting and I decided on the Eagle Scout program."

The Scouts go with him everywhere he goes and listen to almost everything he says. "Every now and then something comes up that's very sensitive, like a criminal investigation, and then I have to excuse them for a while. But other than that, they act just like a member of my own staff."

The day ended with Governor Busbee presenting me with a document bearing the governor's seal, stating that I had participated in the program. My dad and I headed back to Gainesville at the end of the day, my leg throbbing from so much walking. That evening, though, I was at a band rehearsal because we were to play out of town for Thespian Conference dances on Friday and Saturday nights. We played the dates and drove the six hours back to town on Sunday, the day of my Eagle Scout ceremony, when I would finally receive the coveted award that represented many hours of hard work and dedication.

Sunday, February 8, 1981, I received my Eagle Scout award in an evening ceremony at First Baptist Church in Gainesville, along with

five of my peers, including Tim Black, my trusted helper throughout those years. The ceremony was a highly anticipated event, and
many family members and friends were there to share in it with me.
Governor Busbee, whom I had spent the day with just three days earlier, had said that he would like to attend but would be out of town.
His assistant, Tom Purdue, was in attendance, along with his wife.
The ensemble I was in at church sang for the program, and I had a
solo in the song we sang, "Mine Eyes Have Seen the Glory." As a part
of the ceremony, a Scout's mother pins the Eagle pin on the Scout,
and in return, the Scout gives his mother a rose and gives her a pin as
well. My parents had always been there for me, an important part of
the success of all my endeavors, so this was a significant moment for
them as well. Following the meaningful ceremony, there was a reception, where friends and family came to offer their congratulations.
Many people came through the line to offer their well wishes. After
the reception, several family members, including Nanny Rail and
my aunt and uncle Pat and Jerry Rail, along with my cousins, would
come to our house for another time of celebration.

I considered earning my Eagle Scout to be my biggest accomplishment to that point. It was the longest time that I had stuck with
something and completed it. I knew that I had not done it alone,
however. There were many people without whom I could not have
accomplished this milestone, or many of the other things that I had
undertaken.

Not long after my Eagle ceremony, we got word that the national
Scouting magazine wanted to do an article about me. We didn't know
when they would come to do the article but received the call on a
Friday after coming in from a week of vacation over spring break in
Myrtle Beach, South Carolina, that they would come to interview us
that weekend. The article was to be written by Charles Seagraves, and
a photographer was also to be sent to follow us around for three days.
The photographer's name was Manny Rubio, and he had done work
for *Sports Illustrated*, which was really impressive to all my friends.

Saturday was spent at the scout cabin, and the photo op was
for all the Scouts. It seemed that everyone wanted to dress out and
be a part of the photo shoot. Manny got lots of shots of me doing

things like tying knots, showing my fellow Scouts a braille compass, singing and playing guitar, and various activities we normally did. Sunday was spent doing church-related things. Charles and Manny went to our morning services where I sang with the ensemble. More interviews with significant adults in my life and family and friends continued that afternoon. Monday, the two of them followed me to school, doing more of the same with interviewing significant people like Principal Segars and taking photos throughout the day. Everyone wanted to be a part of it, and that again probably helped boost my popularity among my peers. Charles and Manny wanted some shots at home with some friends after taking pictures with friends at school.

They only wanted a few people, and I remember people saying, "Pick me, pick me!" The photographer chose the ones he wanted, and they came to the house later to be photographed with me.

Charles did a good job of capturing the essence of my life and experiences in *Scouting* and would title the article "Mark Dowdy Sings and Soars." He began:

> Back in 1979 Mark Dowdy joined Troop 26 in Gainesville, GA. During the next two years he worked hard, earned 21 merit badges, and performed an uncommonly helpful community service. He became an Eagle Scout, an achievement of no small consequence in such a short time. But it is made all the more extraordinary by the fact that the young man is blind.
>
> Such an achievement is impossible without the proper chemistry. It requires a supportive cast of characters willing to suppress innate fears and overcome tendencies to protect and isolate those who are not quite like the rest of us: parents willing to allow their child to fly, fall and fly again; a Scoutmaster with an understanding of the potential of the blind; and peers who help when asked, but stand in the background when their help is not essential. But most of all it takes a young man with a desire to

realize his potential, to develop his talents, and to overcome what he considers to be a hindrance, not a handicap. Mark Dowdy is such a person. Blind since birth, Mark underwent 13 operations by age 10. Doctors from Atlanta to Boston used state-of-the-art the art technology to try to restore his sight, and one operation proved successful for a short time. Then an irreparable retinal detachment dashed his hopes. Mark now has light perception in one eye, an artificial eye in the other. There is still hope that a new development might restore at least part of his vision, but Mark is not sitting around waiting for that breakthrough. Instead, he is making some breakthroughs of his own.

Charles went on to talk about Troop 26 and my history with the troop:

> Because he happens to be blind, it is necessary to add that he satisfied Eagle requirements "without any special concessions." Spend a few minutes with Mark Dowdy, and you quickly realize how ridiculous it is to have to add that qualifier.
>
> Described by adults who work with him and the friends who know him best as "bright," "talented," "poised," "confident," "charismatic," and "courageous." Mark is all those things. But he prefers to be considered a normal teenager with the same impulsive desires and the same endearments and faults that most teenagers have.

The article also cited what my Eagle project entailed and recounted my earning the marksmanship merit badge:

> Mark has done it all, from hiking, camping, and caving to a day-long canoeing trip down

Arkansas' Buffalo River. He also does his share of camp chores, scrambling eggs by consistency, digging latrines with all the gusto of a mole. He went on to quote Fleming Weaver, "No anxious moments. He's a good swimmer and has a good head on his shoulders. Only he can decide what his limitations are. Believe me, they're few."

My parents concurred, stating in the article,

We have taught ourselves to turn loose, to let him have the freedom to try what he wants to try.

Principal Curtis Segars was interviewed and quoted as saying,

If he steps out of line, I chew his rear out just like any other student, but I have to admit that I don't have to do that too often with Mark.

Charles aptly described Segars in the article:

Segars's flattop haircut and stern exterior could have won him the role of the principal in TV's "Happy Days." He looks as if he stepped right out of the 50s. But his tough exterior belies a deep understanding of the handicapped and a sensitivity to the thousands of students he has served during his 14 years as principal of Gainesville High School. "What can I tell you about Mark Dowdy?" Segars continues. "Well, he's a ham, and like most of our students, he doesn't study enough. But anytime a kid steps out from the crowd in a positive way as Mark has, that's great. He shows what can be done if we'll work at it a little." Segars was not the least bit surprised when a teacher came into his office earlier in the year and exclaimed: "I've seen it all now—Mark Dowdy is leading our new blind student on a tour of the school, showing him where everything is!"

Then Charles wrote a bit about the music and quoted Byron Cutrer:

> He can learn to play any instrument he sets his mind to. He also has a good tenor voice and is blessed with perfect pitch, a gift that few have. Billy Joel has it. Maybe one person in 10,000 has it. With some coaching, his voice will last a long time.

Charles concluded the article by talking about what he perceived to be my acceptance of my blindness:

> He has already developed a seasoned stage presence and an easy rapport with audiences. Humor comes as natural to him as sourness does to a cynic. His humor is never bitter, though at times his acceptance of his blindness is difficult for some to understand. When casting time came for Easter skits, Mark volunteered to play the blind man whose sight was restored by Jesus. It seemed a natural, but he quickly realized that some members of the audience might be uncomfortable with that portrayal. He chose instead to play the dead man who was brought back to life.
>
> "Getting your sight back is one thing," Mark quipped. "But being raised from the dead is something else again. That's what I call some miracle."
>
> To know Mark Dowdy and to see what he has done with his life is inspiring to those who have been lucky enough to earn his friendship. Yet, Mark isn't awed or arrogant about his

achievements thus far. He says simply: "If I can do it, anybody can."

I still believe that if I can do it, anybody can. I love a good underdog story as much as the next guy, probably even more. There is just something about us human beings that causes us to want to root for the most unlikely, the disadvantaged, or the one with seemingly insurmountable obstacles to overcome. For me, there was just no other way but to press on, to give my all to those things most important to me.

Chapter 9

ONE VOICE

The day after we came back from spring break, rehearsals began for *Grease*, the musical with which Pam Ware had baited the hook to get me involved in drama. We had a rigorous rehearsal schedule, practicing on weekends as well as class time and some weeknights. There was a lot going on at one time with rehearsals, some people on the stage, some in the chorus and drama rooms, and other parts of the building—all learning their various parts, which would soon come together for the production. I was amazed at the result when we took the stage and started practicing together. I was slated to be a musician in the band, but closer to the time for the performances, the boy who was to play Johnny Casino was uncast due to getting drunk on a school trip, so I was cast in the role of Johnny Casino. It would be my one and only acting role throughout drama in high school, but for this particular part, it was not much different than a musical performance to me. The Johnny Casino character was a singer and band leader and was prominent in a scene depicting a dance.

I had to go out on stage three different times and announce something about the upcoming music, like, "Just five more minutes till the hand jive contest!"

Then I'd go back out and actually sing the song while others danced in the scene. The actual show ran several nights, and we also went to Gainesville Middle School to perform a portion of the show.

At the same time we were preparing for Grease, our youth choir was preparing a musical called *One Voice*, which we were to perform on Easter Sunday and several days following. Byron Cutrer had written this musical, which had a couple of original songs and other more familiar pieces also. One of the main numbers, and the title of the musical, was based on the Barry Manilow song that was popular at the time, "One Voice." Manilow's recording reportedly had forty-eight tracks of vocals. It started acapella; then by the end was this huge sound comprised of multiple vocal tracks. Byron duplicated that with his arrangement of the song, and he chose me to start the song, I think partly because I didn't need to be given the starting pitch. I sang:

> One voice, singing in the darkness
> All it takes is one voice
> Singing so they hear what's on your mind
> And when you look around you'll find
> There's more than one voice
> Singing in the Darkness
> Joining with your One Voice

Others joined at various places starting with the next line, and by the end, it was a big wall of sound, with the sixty or so young voices joined together.

> Each and every note another octave
> Hands are joined and fears unlocked
> If only One Voice
> Would start it on its own
> We need just one Voice
> Facing the unknown
> And that One Voice
> Would never be alone
> It takes that One Voice
> Just One Voice
> Singing in the darkness
> Shout it out and let it ring
> Just One Voice
> It takes that One Voice
> And everyone will sing

It was a very powerful song done live. I sang rather than played guitar for "One Voice" because we had a paid orchestra that year. Easter Sunday evening was the first performance, and we headed to Pearce Auditorium after Sunday lunch and afternoon visiting at our house with Nanny Rail. Before we left, Nanny had wanted to see some information about the University of Georgia that I received when I went there on a tour to check it out as a possibility for college.

"I don't really have the time to dig the stuff out right now," I said. "I'll show it to you the next time you're here."

It was one of those things I think about now and regret because, little did I know, she would never have that chance. Two days later, my mother found Nanny collapsed on the kitchen floor of Nanny's home. She had been unable to reach Nanny by phone and became concerned, so she went to her house. Nanny had evidently been cooking supper on Monday night when she suffered the massive stroke. The stove was on low, but how it had been on all night and didn't burn the house down is still a mystery. A glass full of tea with melted ice and a plate were on the table, as if she were about to sit down and eat. Nanny was immediately rushed to the hospital, and her prognosis was grim, according to the doctors. We spent the day by her side at the hospital.

Since I had solos in *One Voice*, I went ahead and did the performance that night, even though my heart was heavy. Nanny had been with us and had seen me perform in the musical just two nights before, and I remembered how I put her off about looking at the UGA materials. The next day, the doctors delivered the awful news that Nanny was "brain dead," and shortly after the removal of the respirator, she left this world peacefully. My uncle Jerry, my mother's brother, was also very ill at this time with esophageal cancer.

I had heard Nanny say several times, "I just don't think I can stand to bury my child."

She knew that doctors had told Jerry he only had a short time to live. Nanny had known the heartache of burying a child before when her oldest son, Bobby, had been struck by a car and killed when he was seven years old. My mother, who was not even born at the time, still has some of Bobby's clothes and the school books he was carrying the day he walked to school, when his life was taken from him by the careless man behind the wheel of the car that hit him. Just five weeks after Nanny died, my uncle Jerry would also succumb to the cancer that had wracked his body for months. I remember thinking at the time, and still ponder it today, that God spared Nanny the pain of having to lose another child and took her first. I have no doubt that Nanny and Papa Rail are together, along with Jerry and the other young son, Bobby, whom they had longed to see since he was taken from them all those years ago.

It was a very sad time for all of us, and time seemed to stand still, particularly the week that Nanny passed. In the South, family is everything. Even though we enjoyed lots of friendships and activities with others, life centered primarily around family and those precious relationships. Without the distractions that seem to occupy our time today, extended families tended to focus on one another and be involved in one another's lives to a greater degree. Family really was the tie that would bind, no matter what.

Chapter 10

A Star for Eight Hours

I finished up the tenth grade with all As and one B, considerably better than I had done my freshman year. That summer, I decided I wanted to try and get a job playing at a local restaurant where they had an organ, which was similar to the one I had received as a gift from my parents. I called and made an appointment to go talk to the owner. I was hired on the spot and was to make $5 an hour, twice the minimum wage at the time. In addition to the hourly wage, I also had a tip jar on the organ, which my dad usually "baited" with ten single dollar bills to start each night. It was not unusual for me to make $100 per night in tips, a great deal of money for a fifteen-year-old boy. I would play Thursday, Friday, and Saturday nights from 6:00–10:00 p.m., with two fifteen-minute breaks. I put some of my earnings in savings, but with bulk of the money, I was able to buy some serious musical instruments.

I bought a Les Paul Gold Top guitar, which I kept for a while but then sold. It is one of the instruments I wish I'd held on to because it would be worth thousands of dollars today, but I've always been a "trader," usually wanting the latest and greatest and trading to help get it. I also bought a Hammond B-3 organ, the classic "rock and roll" organ sound heard on so many recordings, new and old. Friends and family would come in to see me play, and since the Beef Corral was one of the few restaurants in town, I knew many of the people who would come to eat. I could take requests, but the only thing I could not play was anything "sacred"—only secular music. During football season, I played every "fight" song imaginable.

It just so happened that my sixteenth birthday, on August 28, was on a Friday that year, and I was slated to play as usual. There was not a lot of fanfare around my sixteenth birthday. I remember the feeling of loneliness as I went to work. My parents, typically ones to make much out of birthdays and Christmas, had given me a shirt for my birthday. They were there with me to eat dinner, but no one else I knew came to see me that night. I remember playing "Happy Birthday" to myself sometime during the evening. My sister had received a car for her sixteenth birthday, and all my friends were getting their licenses. I really felt my blindness that night, and for about a week after that, knowing that I wouldn't be driving like everyone else, getting to taste that freedom which most young boys yearn. Most of my friends had turned sixteen during our tenth-grade year, and I had watched them all gain the independence that comes with the use of a car. Even so, this didn't have much of an effect on me somehow until I was sixteen, and that night I felt like I didn't have anything to look forward to.

This time was also the beginning of "dating" for most of my friends, and I was realizing the difficulty in dating as well. I had many friends who were girls, but if it ever looked like it would turn into a dating situation, they were gone. There were several girls that I wanted to date, and I was surprised, shocked, and even angered each time I experienced rejection. Sometimes I would make plans with a girl, but at the last minute, she would cancel or just not show up. It seemed, though, that the rejection would always push me back into the music. I would spend time practicing and playing rather than going out like many of my friends were doing at that point. I tried not to spend too much time dwelling on things I could not change, however, and attempted to focus on the positive.

It was in the fall of the year that my next band, Tempest, was formed as a result of a couple of buddies of mine and I playing for a class at the request of a teacher. Friends Tim Davidson, Mike Johnson, and I formed the group along with Rusty Baker, who played bass. We practiced at Tim's house in his basement, and soon we had a set list and felt we were ready to play out somewhere. Our first opportunity to play was for Gainesville High School Marching Band's Christmas party. It was held at the Civic Center in Gainesville every year. They paid us $100 to play, which really legitimized the band as far as we were concerned. Word spread, and we had the opportunity to play for a New Year's Eve party for Gainesville Park and Recreation Agency a couple of weeks later. Our parents went in together and bought a PA system that we used when we played.

We were getting quite a following and were playing out at least once a month. We felt that with our newfound fame, it was time to make a "fashion statement" and do something which at the time was bold and daring: we were going to get our ears pierced. Tim Davidson and I left school during third period one day to go to Merle Norman at Lakeshore Mall across the street to make our dreams a reality. They had a special going for $20, and since Tim and I just needed the one ear pierced, they let us pay $20 and split the pair of earrings. Of course, we chose gold star earrings, a symbol befitting our newfound fame.

We went back to school with our new status symbols, where we heard comments like, "Wow, cool—you got your ear pierced!"

My math teacher, Mrs. Charlotte Ridgeway, took one look at me and said, "Your mama is gonna kill you, and I'd love to be there to see it!"

Not long after we returned to school, it started snowing, and we were released early. Any hint of a snowflake in the south, and schools let out quicker than you can say "gravy and biscuits." Tim dropped me by home, and I did my best to avoid my mother that afternoon, or at least turn my left side from her as much as I could. Finally, though, she noticed the earring and just started laughing.

"You just wait till your daddy gets home!" she said.

When my dad came home from work, I did my best to steer clear of him. However, that night at supper, there was no getting around it.

"Bobby, how do you like Mark's new addition?" my mother finally said, after my dad didn't seem to notice anything.

My dad started laughing too!

"I guess it's okay. Evidently, you're ready to start supporting yourself?" he asked me.

"What do you mean?" I asked innocently.

"If you're going to keep that, you're going to be supporting yourself."

He strongly encouraged me to take it off then and there, but the back proved difficult to remove, no matter how hard I tried.

"I'll get it off there," he said with determination.

It wouldn't yield to him either, however, until he employed the use of a small pair of pliers. He yanked and pulled at my then painful ear, until the back came off and the "star" fell. Tim fared better and was allowed to keep his earring for a while, but I only had a "star" for about eight hours.

Chapter 11

NASHVILLE BOUND

Not long after the earring fiasco, I was at Rusty Baker's house for band practice, and while we were waiting on others to arrive, I was sitting at the piano in the living room playing and singing. Rusty's mother was on the phone in the kitchen, talking to her brother, who happened to be in the music business. His name was Bobby Wood, and he was quite accomplished, having played on some of the early Elvis Presley records in Memphis. He was originally from Mississippi but had moved to Nashville and had experienced success as a studio musician and songwriter. He wrote and played on Crystal Gayle hits like "Don't It Make My Brown Eyes Blue, and "You've Been Talkin' in Your Sleep," among others. He had been on the *Tonight Show,* which was impressive to all of us and also owned a publishing company located on the famed Music Row in Nashville.

As he and Rusty's mother talked, he was hearing me in the background and asked, "Who is that playing and singing?"

Rusty's mother began to tell him about me, and to all of our surprise, he asked to speak with me.

"I want you to call Ed Sey at Webb Four studios in Atlanta. Tell him you need to make a two-track demo, and when you get it done, I want you to come and see me in Nashville," he told me.

Following our conversation, I was on cloud nine and couldn't believe what had just happened. I went home and told my parents, and they were floored as well, but soon made the arrangements with the studio in Atlanta for me to make my first recording.

So on February 18, we headed to Webb Four Studios, which was one of the premier studios in Atlanta at the time. It had been built in the 1970s and had a real '70s vibe about it, right down to the dark paneling covering the walls. The studio was in an old warehouse, and the entrance went right into the "live" room, which was a huge area with high ceilings and a drum platform in the middle of the room. The control room was at the back of the studio, and it was complete with all kinds of gear. It was a 5:00 p.m. session, the last one of the day, and we had the studio booked for two hours. Back then, the studio went for $100 per hour, plus the musician costs. It was that day that I met Tommy Cooper, a twenty-four-year-old engineer who had graduated from the University of Georgia with a degree in journalism but would never work as a journalist. Having an intense interest in recording, he landed a position at Webb Four as an assistant. His first project was a Melissa Manchester album, and he would go on to be the main engineer on projects for Melissa Manchester, Lionel Richie and the Commodores, Paul Davis, and Isaac Hayes, among others. He had only been engineering for a couple of years but was very competent and confident in what he did. Tommy had been responsible for lining up the players for drums, bass and guitar, with me on the piano. Tommy and I developed an immediate rapport, and he seemed to enjoy working with me during the session.

The recording itself was a two-track recording, so the instruments and vocal were recorded at once, and there was no "punching" in and out to fix anything. I had not begun to write songs at that point and chose to do all cover tunes. I sang "Lady" by Kenny Rogers, "Just the Way You Are" and "She's Got a Way" by Billy Joel, "Three Times a Lady" by the Commodores," and "Rise Again" by Dallas Holm. I chose to sing and play "She's Got a Way" with just the piano, so it was a little different from the others. I fell in love with the recording process that day, even though my time there was very limited, and I remember thinking, *I've got to find a way to do this all the time!* I recall the first time that day that I sat behind the console, right in the middle, and heard my playback. I was just in awe of the whole thing and thought it was the most amazing experience of my life to that point. I was excited to see what the future would hold and what Bobby Wood's opinion would be of the recording.

With the demo completed, we planned our trip to Nashville for the first weekend in March to meet Bobby Wood and learn what our next step should be. In a large van borrowed from family friends, we loaded up for the trip Friday morning: my mom, dad, Rusty's mom, Rusty, and also a girl who was singing with our band, Elaine Rogers, and myself. We arrived in Nashville at Bobby's house about noon on Friday. It turned out that Bobby and his wife rolled out the red carpet for us and had many activities planned for our visit. He was anxious to hear the recording, however; and after some initial pleasantries, he loaded up the reel in a "music room" in his house and gave us his assessment.

"Yeah, it's good. It's not going to happen for you right away, though, but it's a good start," he said.

He gave me some good advice that I really took to heart and tried to learn from.

"You're overplaying—you're all over the place. You need to learn to play with the rest of the band," he said truthfully.

I could see his point. I was used to performing by myself and trying to be "the band" with just the guitar or piano. Learning not to overplay when playing with a band is something that good musicians usually learn with time.

"I want to keep up with you and track your progress," he said.

One of Bobby's concerns was that I would "peak" too soon. He explained that at that time, the average artist had a span of about five to seven years where he or she would remain relevant and then sort of fade into the background. I was sixteen, and he didn't want to see me with a career as a recording artist that would last only into my early twenties.

Bobby and his wife treated us like family during the whole trip, and he surprised Rusty and me when he offered to let us ride around Nashville that afternoon in his Triumph TR7. Later in the day, they took us around Nashville, doing some of the typical tourist things, but Bobby had a couple of surprises up his sleeve. He had arranged for us to spend some time at Birdsong Studios, which was one of the most prestigious studios in Nashville at that time, with many of the big hits of the day being recorded there. Bobby wanted to see me in that setting and hear me sing and play in the studio environment. It was the highlight of the trip for me and confirmed my love for the studio.

We toured Bobby's office on Music Row and then topped the day off with grilling hamburgers at Bobby's house. As was typical for that time of year, it had gone from being warm during the day to a big temperature drop toward the evening. I had not brought a jacket because it was warm when we left home. Bobby went to his closet and pulled out a handmade leather jacket complete with fringe, the kind that was popular then, for me to wear that evening. When we got ready to leave for the hotel, I was pulling the jacket off to give back to him.

"Why don't you just take that home with you?" he said, to my astonishment.

I knew the jacket would have been a very expensive piece of clothing. I expressed my thanks, again filled with a sense of awe about the whole experience. We left Nashville the next morning, me armed with information that I could use for the future, my dreams fueled by the surreal experiences of the weekend.

Chapter 12

Driving Blind

No retelling of my story would be complete without revealing some of the more foolish and dangerous activities in which I sometimes engaged. During my late teenage years, I encountered several friends who, at various times, gave me the opportunity to feel the thrill of being behind the wheel. It was around the fall of 1982 that I developed a friendship with a guy that was a year older than I was. He had graduated the year before, and I was a senior in high school. He had a Mazda RX-7 with a manual transmission, and I wanted to learn to drive it. So being teens and risk takers, we devised a plan for me to do just that. We began going to empty parking lots for me to get the feel of the stick shift and stopping/starting. I remember the excitement and suppressed terror that gripped me as I sat behind the wheel for the first time in that parking lot.

After we both felt I had sufficiently mastered the gears and gas/brake in the parking lot, we decided it was time to try my skills on the open road. Foolishly, we chose a place in Gainesville that teenagers called Thrill Hill. Terrain is hilly in our part of Georgia, but this particular road was especially steep. It seemed like it went straight down and straight back up again, and teens would go down the hill at top speed, almost going airborne at the dip before going up again. The boldness of youth must have told us that it would be a good idea to put the blind guy behind the wheel.

I took the wheel at the beginning of Ledan Road, and although the speed limit was 45 mph, we were soon going about 70 mph. We hit the dip going top speed and, sure enough, felt the thrill of the car lifting off the ground slightly as we headed up the hill on the other side. As teenage minds think, we reasoned that if once was good, twice would be even better. We turned around and took the hill again, feeling the thrill of speed and rush that comes with doing something dangerous. It was on the fourth run that trouble found us in the form of a police officer who happened to know my family well. The blue lights flashed, and we pulled over, my friend Joe helping to guide me to the edge of the road. The officer came to the window, and I rolled it down. I don't know if it would have been better if he had not known me, but he expressed his complete surprise at seeing me in the driver's seat.

"Man, I am not believin' this. If it had been anybody else, I would have put you *under* the jail! How am I going to go back and explain this?"

I was hoping that because he knew me, he would see the humor in it, but he went on to lecture us quite loudly about the danger we'd put ourselves and others in on that road and how stupid it was on so many levels. He told us to change places immediately and that he'd better not ever catch us doing that again, threatening to tell our fathers as well.

The stern warning and the mercy he extended to us made an impact on me, but not quite enough to keep me from driving several more times during this period in my life. About six months after the Thrill Hill incident, I had another friend, Chris, who was brave enough to let me try driving on the interstate. Again we devised a plan, doing some driving around the community college after hours, learning how to stop at stop signs, slowing down and accelerating at the proper times in his Mustang GT with an automatic transmission. After he felt I had sufficiently mastered the timing, we decided to go on the interstate, Chris in the seat on the right with his hand on the steering wheel as well, ready to make corrections as needed. I can remember again feeling something similar to the time I flew down Thrill Hill as we accelerated up the ramp to the interstate. We went slowly up the ramp and were then on the open road. We ended up going a couple of exits down and pulled into a convenience store to get gas and snacks. This was at the time gas stations still had attendants who would pump the gas for you. We pulled up to the pump slowly, with Chris guiding the car. We got out to walk into the store, and I went around the front of the car to wait for Chris to guide me into the store. As we exited the car and I moved around to Chris, the attendant could obviously tell that I could not see. Chris said the attendant just shook his head.

"Now I've seen everything," he said.

I guess we freaked him out, but hopefully he had a story to tell his family later that night! We did that type of interstate driving several times, sometimes going for long stretches, once even heading down I-75 toward Florida. We always went at night when there was less traffic, and there were fewer cars on the road in general back then. Also, my night vision was better because I could see headlights and traffic lights against the background of the night more easily, making it the best time to try such a thing. We had discussed the matter and determined it was not likely we would get caught as long as we didn't go fast or do anything to call attention to ourselves—it all made perfect sense to us. Of course, our actions were immensely foolish, and I thank God no one got hurt as a result of it. But we never did get pulled over on any of those excursions. Looking back, I see all the more how the good Lord was surely watching over me during the dangerous things I did in my youth!

Graham, Michelle, Mark, Macy

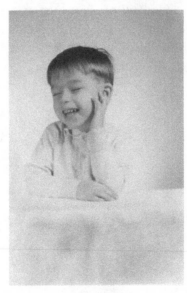

Mark age 2

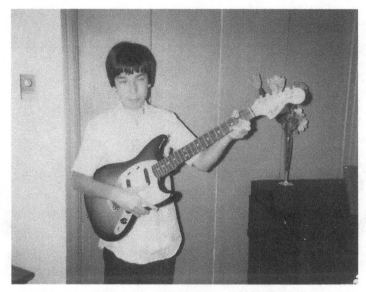

Mark age 10

Mark and Graham

Mark and his parents at Eagle Scout Ceremony

Mark and Macy

Mark performing age 10

Mark plays toy piano

Chapter 13

A Strange Turn of Events

While I had been hopeful, nothing came of the recording of the demos in Nashville, besides feedback from Bobby and the experience that it provided for me. Life returned to its normal pace with all its ups and downs when I returned home. The band I was in broke up at the end of my junior year, amid disagreement on the style of music we wanted to do. In the middle of my senior year of high school, an event happened that took all of us by surprise. On a Sunday morning in January of '83, Byron Cutrer announced to the First Baptist Church that he would be leaving us. Nobody had seen it coming. He had been such a big part of my development; he was my mentor, both musically and spiritually. I was devastated, along with so many others from our group. Byron did a farewell concert, and it was a tough thing to get through. I played, and Byron did most of the singing. It was the first time since the death of my grandparents that I'd felt such a sense of loss. I remember Byron and his family driving out of the church parking lot, and we all just stood there in a daze. It was profound sadness, like I'd lost my direction, and something I had relied on was gone forever. In my teenage mind, I wondered how I'd move on without his influence in my life. But as with all things, life does move us onward following a loss.

It was time for me to begin thinking about my schooling beyond my high school career. I knew I wanted a career in music but was sure I did not want to teach. In spite of not knowing exactly what I wanted to do, I auditioned at Belmont College in Nashville in February. I was accepted into the program but was not offered any scholarship money. It was a very expensive school, $8,000 per year, which was a great deal of money at that time. The thought of going away to college and the challenges it would pose did not bother me. I knew I could handle the challenge the same way I had faced down other obstacles in my life. I had also applied at Berkley in Boston.

During my senior year, I had been joint enrolled in what was then Gainesville College and my high school. After my Belmont audition and realizing the additional burden the cost would put on our family, I reasoned that the best thing to do would be to continue at the community college where I was already enrolled. The cost per quarter at Gainesville College was a mere $207, and I did receive a music scholarship there. I really applied myself to my studies in a way that I had not done in high school, and after my first quarter there, I was called into my advisor's office and told I qualified for an academic scholarship as well.

"Are you sure you have the right person?" I asked nervously.

They were sure, and I ended up not paying anything for my education at Gainesville College beyond that point. Despite doing well academically, I found some of the music classes most challenging. I double-majored in music and psychology, and every music major was required to take private voice and piano lessons. Ms. Frances Brown taught both, and I knew after the first two piano lessons that I was in trouble. I had already been playing piano for a few years, but I was self-taught, and my fingering was all wrong. We started with learning scales. After a couple of rough lessons, Miss Frances said to me, "Maybe you'd better just drop this class because you can't play the piano." I was hurt by it at first but tried not to let it deter me. I knew I could play, just not with the techniques I was required to use in those lessons. I went to one of the other music professors, who was my advisor, and told him what had happened. He doubled me up on conducting and ear training, and I was able to drop the piano lessons. I also had a hard time with theory. Up until that point, I did everything by ear and was able to get by without knowing much theory. As it so happened there was a girl in my theory class that I had been all the way through school with, and she graciously agreed to tutor me. She spent a lot of time with me that year, even coming to my house to give me extra help. The theory was definitely something I would use later in working with bands, choirs, and studio musicians.

In the fall of '83, my freshman year in college, I felt it was time for me to get back to the studio, and I shared this with my parents. I also had two songwriters encouraging me to do so. John Jarrard had begun to have some success in Nashville at that point, and another local songwriter, Connolly White, had a deal with Tree Publishing. I knew both of them fairly well, and they encouraged me to update my demo.

"You need to get to Nashville, but you need to go back to Webb Four and cut some new material. I'm sure your voice has changed a lot in two years," advised John.

So the plans were made for me to again record at Webb Four, this time with original songs. Since the time I had recorded my first demos, I had also facilitated a couple of other sessions for people who wanted to record, really acting as a producer but not even being aware of what a producer did. I would set everything up, find musicians, and play on the session myself, more or less leading the session. I worked with Tommy Cooper on all the occasions that I worked at Webb Four and relied on his guidance as well. When I returned to cut my second set of demos, he commented that I had come a long way as a player since those first demos. I wasn't stepping all over the band; I had settled down a little. The demos were completed in October, and we sat on them a couple of months because things were so busy around that time. I did send the tapes to John Jarrard, and in January, he called me with an idea.

"I've got somebody I want to see if I can hook you up with to produce your next music," he said.

That person was Billy Strange, well-known then and now to most anybody in the music industry. In less than two weeks from that phone call, on a cold day in February, we boarded a plane to Nashville to meet with the famous Billy Strange. As it turned out, Billy had the stomach flu and had tried to contact us before we left but didn't catch us in time. It was long before the days of cell phones, so we arrived in Nashville not knowing that he was really ill. He met with us in spite of feeling so badly and had to excuse himself several times throughout the afternoon. Billy had moved to Nashville in the '70s and was a proficient session guitarist and songwriter and, despite his successes, was a very unassuming person. He had written songs for Elvis Presley ("A Little Less Conversation") and Chubby Checker ("Limbo Rock"). Billy had recorded with Elvis Presley, Nat King Cole, and was single-handedly responsible for the guitar sound on recordings of the Beach Boys. He also produced and played the famous guitar solo associated with the James Bond movie theme music and arranged Nancy Sinatra's number one pop hit, "These Boots Are Made for Walkin'." Not until years later, and actually recently through a book called *The Wrecking Crew*, did I actually learn the full extent of Billy's accomplishments.

In addition to producing and creating a wide range of music, Billy was helping young artists along who were introduced to him in some way by trusted friends or industry acquaintances. We met at his house, which was like a typical middle-class home of the day, in Franklin, Tennessee. We initially spent some time talking about the music business, *Billboard* magazine, and how the charts are done. Billy had heard my demo and said he heard a lot of potential in it. After some discussion, we went downstairs where Billy had an upright piano.

"Play," he said simply.

I sat down at the piano and played and sang for about twenty minutes. He stood over me, watching and listening intently as I sang. When I finished he said, "Well, one thing is clear—you've got it. You've got what it takes to make it. I'd like to produce you. I'd like to cut four sides to equal two singles."

He told us he would start sending me material to review for the singles. About a week after our trip, I started receiving packets in the mail from him, almost every day, packed with cassette-tape demos for me to review. I listened to about one hundred songs to get the four that we used. As I was going through the material, some songs I liked and some I didn't care for at all. There was one song that I came across that I really wanted to do, but Billy put the brakes on it.

"Absolutely not. It has too much of a pop feel—too much like Lionel Ritchie," he said wisely.

I really held out for doing the song, and Billy was very patient with me, even though the answer was no. I guess he knew I was eighteen and thought I knew everything; but in reality, I didn't know much of anything about the music business yet. Around this same time, John Jarrard was also sending me material. John was writing for Maypop Music at that time, a division of Alabama. I ended up using two of John's songs: "Good Thing Going" and "Follow Your Heart," cowritten with Keith Steigel, who has produced Alan Jackson, Zac Brown Band, and many others.

About a month after our initial meeting with Billy, we were in the studio in Nashville recording the four songs. The studio environment in Nashville was very different than in Atlanta.

Man, I've hit the big time! I thought.

We recorded in a new studio called Star Gem and used all A-lister musicians: David Humphries on drums, Tony Migliore on keys, David Hungate (original Toto member) on bass, Peter Bordinelli on guitar. It was during these sessions that I began to realize what a real producer did as I watched Billy guide the whole process and give his input to every aspect of the recording. Even then, during my attempts to be a recording artist, I was becoming enamored with the production process, and the seeds were sown for what would later become my real aspiration and the direction my career would take.

Chapter 14

Billboard Picks and
Reality Checks

The four songs were recorded, and Billy seemed very pleased with the end result. We released the first single, "Lady Afraid to Let Go," to radio. In August of 1984, I received a call from Billy saying that we'd hit *Billboard* magazine as one of the "picks" for the month. I remember immediately trying to find a copy of *Billboard* magazine in Gainesville, Georgia, which was no easy task. We finally found a copy at one of the local radio stations that played music, WGGA. Terry Barnhart, one of the on-air personalities at the time, was kind enough to give us the copy. Billy was encouraged and began thinking about what the next single would be. We decided on "Follow Your Heart," and it was released in November of 1984. In December, we again hit *Billboard* as one of the picks. People were saying this was very unusual for a young independent artist to have two *Billboard* picks in a row and were telling Billy, "You've really got something here."

We were trying to capitalize on the notoriety I was gaining as result of the *Billboard* picks, and I was singing as much as I could while at the same time playing in a band and going to school. The local paper did an article titled, "Dowdy Hopes He's Got a 'Good Thing Going,'" which let the community know what was going on. I did a concert in the spring of that year at Pearce Auditorium in Gainesville, our premier local venue, putting a band together and rehearsing them for about six weeks. It was a great night, and we performed the singles I had recorded plus some cover tunes.

Billy was excited about the *Billboard* picks but, around the same time, had signed on to work with Marty Haggard, son of Merle Haggard, one of country music's greats. They were trying to work out a deal for Marty at MTM Records. MTM was Mary Tyler Moore's company, and they had come to Nashville, putting their extensive resources into the new company, whose goal was to get into country music. As things progressed, Billy began to put more of his energies into Marty's career, and I was pushed to the back burner. I felt like it was because Marty had the name recognition, and maybe Billy felt Marty had a better chance at making it in the music business as a recording artist. I couldn't blame Billy for the turn of events because I knew he had to look out for his own interests.

After not receiving the continued support from Billy that I needed, I started to become disillusioned with my own recording career. At the same time, I was becoming more interested in the process of recording and began to learn all I could about the Fostex 4 track machine I had received for Christmas. I was learning how to record and make demos with the new equipment, further honing the skills that would help me to make a living in the music business in the future. By December of 1984, I had earned enough college credits to graduate with my associate's degree, having been joint-enrolled my senior year in high school. The world was calling, and I was ready for the next step, even though I was not sure exactly what that would be.

In June of '85, I had the opportunity to audition for a group called the Fort Mountain Boys. This group was made up of six "good old boys," two of whom were twin brothers, who had been together for five years. They were known for opening up for the big-name country stars of the day, and they were looking for a keyboard player. My friend Chris Pope and I had taken some lighting equipment to a concert venue in Hiawassee, Georgia, where Conway Twitty was the main attraction, and the Fort Mountain Boys were the opening act. Chris worked for OAP, a sound and lighting company that had a contract with the music hall in Hiawassee. When we met the members of the Fort Mountain Boys and found out they were looking for a keyboard player, Chris offered me up on the spot.

"My friend here plays," he said.

Particularly after hearing about my recent success with the singles, they immediately wanted to hear me play and worked it out with Conway Twitty's keyboard player for me to play the Yamaha CP-80, which was like a mini-grand piano, in between the Fort Mountain Boys' set and Conway Twitty's. I sat down and played, and they all gathered around and sang. It was a favorable reaction, and they invited me back to sit in with them during a rehearsal. They took a vote that night and asked me on site if I wanted to go on the road with them. I was not a band member, just a contract player, but I ended up going everywhere with them for about six months. We would be gone five to seven days at a time, traveling all over the country, and then return for a couple of days at home. I'd do my laundry and then load up and start it all over again. We opened up for all the country greats of the day: George Jones, Tanya Tucker, Lee Greenwood, Conway Twitty, and many more.

One of the highlights—or, as it turned out, maybe it was more like "lowlights"—was when we played on a cruise where Tanya Tucker was the main act. My parents, grandmother, and some aunts and uncles decided they wanted to go on this trip, many of them having never been on a cruise. Little did we know at the time the bookings were made that we would have to sail straight through a hurricane just hours into the cruise. Nearly everyone on board, including myself, was seasick from the violent lurching of the ship—everyone, that is, except my ninety-year-old grandmother, who seemed to endure it all with no ill effects. The ship rocked and bobbed for eighteen hours, but then mercifully we made it through the eye of the hurricane to the other side and were able to continue with the shows and other fun activities of the cruise.

On that cruise in particular, I saw the seedy side of country music, with drugs and drinking seemingly the main recreational activity for some of the musicians. It is no secret that Tanya Tucker lived that kind of lifestyle as well, and I was seeing it firsthand. I wondered how some of the musicians could even play after they had consumed so many mind-altering substances. One night, my uncle Elwood had an interesting encounter with Tanya Tucker in the hallway of the ship when she was clearly inebriated. Uncle Elwood had driven a truck for many years for Roadway and was a short balding, unassuming kind of man who was as country as a dirt road. For some unknown reason, Tanya Tucker ran down the hall and jumped into Elwood's arms, straddling him with her legs and an enthusiasm that I'm sure put a strain on poor Elwood's heart. We never quite knew what had prompted this unexpected show of affection, but Elwood clearly got a kick out of it, although my aunt Doris was quite put off by the whole thing! The cruise was full of exciting times, and all my family survived, but most vowed never to go on another one.

Life on the road was definitely not all glitz and glamour, though; and while the Fort Mountain Boys played some high-profile venues, we also played some "dives" and small gigs along the way to the bigger ones. My first experience with one of these gigs was a bar where there was chicken wire in front of the stage area.

"What's the chicken wire for?" I naively asked the bar manager.

"Oh, you'll find out about ten o'clock," was his reply.

I did indeed find out around that hour when the fights started to break out and the bottles started flying, the chicken wire being our only protection against the onslaught. With all these experiences—the good, the bad, and the ugly——fresh in my mind, I began to be introspective about my life and where I was headed. I knew I wanted my music to count for something, and I knew I didn't like a lot of what I was seeing out on the road. I started entertaining the idea of producing more and maybe even opening a studio of my own someday.

I left the Fort Mountain Boys following the cruise in late 1985 after becoming disillusioned with that aspect of the music business. It was then that I met Dede Fowler, whose sister Kim was dating one of the Fort Mountain Boys. Dede was a good singer and wanted to explore songwriting. She was about four years older than I was, and we decided to try and write together. It was my first experience with cowriting. Over the course of the next year, we wrote together regularly and put together a catalog of songs. In January of 1986, we decided we would take a trip to Nashville, with the plan being to "set the world on fire" with our newly written material. We thought we'd simply walk in, pitch these great songs, get a great contract, get rich, etc., and the rest would be history. So with a few songs we'd written and some really crude demos I'd recorded in my basement with a 4-track recorder, Dede, her mom, and I set off for Nashville in an RV that her parents owned.

It was a cold winter, and we stayed in that RV at a campground near Nashville and rented a car to get around town in during the day. We stayed in Nashville for a week. In the morning, we would go down to the Shoney's Inn on Music Row, eat breakfast, and get our game plan together. Our first order of business was to go to the NSAI (Nashville Songwriter's Association International) offices and get a directory of publishers. We used the directory to cold-call publishers and try to set up appointments. We actually did make some good appointments, and looking back now, I am surprised at how many people actually agreed to see us and give our songs a listen. We went around town pitching those songs, thinking we had written the best stuff since "The Long and Winding Road." We had meetings all week long. Everyone was nice and cordial, but no one was buying. We had scheduled a meeting with John Jarrard later in the week for him to take a listen to our stuff and offer some feedback. He gave it in his candid, dry, honest way.

"Man, this is better than what I was writing at your age—but, man, it's not good," he said with painful honesty.

Since John was one that had been instrumental in getting me to Nashville and in helping me make connections, I knew he had my best interest at heart. That was a good gut check for me; I knew I had a long way to go. As it turns out, though, something good did come out of the trip for us. About six months later, we were informed by one of the publishers we'd visited that Crystal Gayle and Gary Morris wanted to cut one of our songs for a duet album for Candlelight Music. It was my first cut, and my first royalty check was for that song, "Through Your Eyes."

Dede and I continued to write songs on and off for the next several months, but the production bug was still biting. My dad and

I had been discussing the fact that I needed to improve my recording setup and needed more tracks on which to record. In March, my dad went down to Metro Music and bought an 8-track recorder. I had no idea that he was going to do it that day. A couple of weeks later, we went back and got the larger mixer that went with the recorder. I set it up in my basement and started recording anything and everything and everybody I could. It was a good experience. I had doubled my tracks and gone from cassette tape to reel to reel, so the quality was a lot better. That small setup was a great stepping-stone to even bigger things.

It was in the spring/summer of '86 that I really began to feel the pull of wanting my music to count for something, and I just wasn't seeing that pay off with country music at that time. I felt prompted to focus on writing music with Christian lyrics. The first "Christian" song I wrote was a song called "The Wonder of It All." It was entered in a BMI (Broadcast Music Inc.) songwriter's contest, and it won! I went to Nashville and performed the song at the ceremony at BMI headquarters. That small victory confirmed to me that I was on the right path, so I started writing more songs. I wrote songs called "Forever Love" and "Life of the World," which also won BMI contests.

The year 1986 was pivotal. It was in the summer of the year that I would make an acquaintance who would change my life forever. One Saturday, a good buddy of mine, Hugh Norman, and I were hanging out together. We decided to go to a local music store and check out some of their keyboard equipment. They had a clavinet that I had heard about and had wanted to audition. Working at the store that day was a girl I had not met before. Michelle Morlock had just graduated from high school and had been in Hugh Norman's choir and youth group at Blackshear Place Baptist Church, where he was a summer intern. She would be heading to college in the fall of that year. Hugh introduced me to Michelle when we entered, and we spent some time in the store playing some of the keyboards and looking around at music. I bought a couple of cassette tapes, and Michelle rang me up at the register. I thought she was friendly and pleasant but didn't think any more about it following our initial meeting.

Later that year in November, Michelle's dad, Ray, called me because Michelle wanted to do an audition tape for the group Truth. Someone he worked with gave him my name. Michelle had a friend who had been in the group and was going to pass the tape along to Roger Breland, who had started the group. Truth was often a springboard to bigger opportunities for young aspiring artists.

Plans were made for Michelle to come and record a few songs, and she showed up at my house at ten o'clock in the morning one Friday for our scheduled session. I opened the door, and we spoke our hellos and initial pleasantries. In that very moment—I kid you not—I had the most irrational thought.

This is the girl I'm going to marry.

Michelle had brought accompaniment tracks of what she wanted to record. I told her I usually just played all the instruments and didn't normally use accompaniment tracks to record. I learned later that she was highly dubious of my claim but was much too polite to express any doubts to me at the time. We did record using her accompaniment tracks, which, of course, didn't take nearly as much time as if I had made the tracks. We would talk in between takes, and it still ended up taking most of the day. She was easy to be with, and we really seemed to hit it off. I was sorry to see her walk out the door when she left. She said she would let me know how everything worked out and if anything came of sending the tape to Mr. Breland. I wished her luck, and she was on her way. I didn't know how or when, but I knew I would see her again.

Chapter 15

Producer Hat

Around this same time, I met a young lady, Christie Dykes, who would be the first artist for whom I would produce an entire record. She was from Dothan, Alabama, but had family in Gainesville. She sang at First Baptist Church on a Sunday in August, which was where I first heard her. There was a quality about her voice that I liked, and I was impressed. She was attending Samford University at the time and had been first runner up in the Miss Alabama pageant the previous year. I went up and spoke to her after the service and found out she would be singing again in the evening service. She had sung to an accompaniment track that morning but really wanted someone to play for her live. We decided to practice in the afternoon and put something together for that evening, so I ended up playing for her in the evening service. We seemed to "click," and following the service, we went to a pizza place to discuss possible plans for a future recording, and then back to my house to listen to some demos I had recorded that might be suitable for her album.

About a week later, Christie's father and I settled on a "deal" and a plan for getting the project done. We had decided first to do a single (side A and side B) and try to promote it on Christian radio, with plans to complete the project if things went well. I immediately began calling musicians to set up the recording session at Webb Four and again called on Tommy Cooper to engineer. We recorded two songs I had recently written, "Forever Love" and "Life of the World," and "Forever Love" was released as a single to radio. It started doing well on the charts as an independent production, and once again I felt I was on the right path.

I remember thinking, *Okay, I can't NOT do this!*

I knew that if I were going to produce, the obvious thing would be for me to have my own studio; that was the natural progression. After much discussion, my dad agreed to put up the money to finance the equipment, and we started looking around for space to buy or rent. We looked at a space that had been a doctor's office and other old buildings, one of which had been a teen dance club.

During '86, I was also doing some work for Home Federal, the bank my Dad had worked for since 1963. The CEO and founder of this bank was a giant of a man in our community named James Mathis. It is well known that it was James Mathis who helped to make our community what it is today. He was a true visionary, ahead of his time in so many ways. He and my dad had always worked closely together, so I had grown up knowing him. I was what he called his "special projects coordinator." He was full of creative ideas, and I would be called in to help him execute his plans. He had rocking chairs in his office and would frequently call me into the inner sanctum.

"Come rock with me a few minutes, and let's talk about an idea I have," he'd say.

The projects ranged from advertising /promotional ideas to radio spots and jingles to planning community events. Sometimes I would help write scripts with someone in the marketing department and then go to the radio station and record the voiceovers for the spots for advertising campaigns. At one point, Mr. Mathis decided he wanted to link up all of the offices with the same music and intercom system, and I oversaw all of that.

Not long after I'd finished the singles for Christie, Mr. Mathis called my dad at home one night.

"Y'all meet me up at the building. I want to talk to you about something," he said with excitement in his voice.

Home Federal had purchased an old building that used to be a Kroger grocery store, adjacent to the main branch and offices. It was a huge building, and they were using a portion of it for a gym and kitchen for the employees. It was this building that Mr. Mathis was talking about, and we immediately went to meet him there.

"I've got an idea," he began as he unlocked the door for us to enter.

I had learned that anytime he said, "I've got an idea," either it was going to be impossible to pull off or the best idea you'd ever heard. The impossible to pull off usually meant you did it anyway, but as it turned out, this was one of the "best ideas you've ever heard" kind of thing.

"Mark, I know you want to produce and record things for folks, and I know there would be a lot of unknowns about renting a space to try and do that. I want to offer you some space in this building, rent-free," he said.

I was blown away with the offer and the idea. That night, we went around with a sharpie and a tape measure, marking off space and talking out what we would need for adequate room for a studio. Plans were soon underway to get started and enclose the space needed. We enlisted the help of my cousin Tony, who had taken over my uncle Jerry's construction business, although we did some of the work ourselves to save on cost. We also had to choose equipment and decide on who would install it. It took about three months to complete from the time Mr. Mathis made the proposal, and we were up and running by the time we were ready for the rest of Christie's album to be recorded.

When the space was ready and the equipment had been installed, we asked Tommy Cooper to come up and spend the day with me to help me learn about the new equipment with which I was unfamiliar. Tommy was then teaching engineering at the Music Business Institute of Atlanta (MBI). After spending the day with me, Tommy suggested that I might want to take some classes from MBI to gain some more knowledge. I was able to use my own studio as a lab, so I didn't have the inconvenience of having to get to Atlanta. I didn't care about receiving credit for the classes; I just wanted to have the knowledge to hone my craft. I went through the classes, with Tommy guiding me, him listening to things I would send to him and offering his honest and helpful critiques. Tommy helped me understand what I was doing and how to do things the right way. I learned about everything from how to mic things, to the physics of sound, to psychoacoustics, and more. Even to this day, I will still send things to Tommy for his opinion.

I completed Christie's project in the new studio, playing all the instruments myself for the rest of the project. I was also taking on other projects, and the studio was quite busy that first year of operation. I soon learned, however, that I had to record all kinds of music in order to keep things going. There are a lot of people out there who want to record, and every one of them thinks he or she can be a "star." In those days, I took anything I could, even recording a "good ol' boy" who came down from the mountains, usually drunk, to record demos for songs he'd written. He was probably in an inebriated state when he wrote the following lyrics:

> I've got a cat named Ruff
> And a dog named Mouse
> I've got a lake in my kitchen
> So I can go fishin' when it rains
> I've got alligators in my bathtub
> And buffalos on my wall

In addition to the colorful lyrics, "Tom" (name changed to protect the guilty) would play the guitar in a different key than he was singing in. I remember trying to tune his guitar for him, thinking that might help, but then coming to the realization that it didn't make any difference. I would sit in the control room with the monitors almost all the way down and try to keep my composure. He would sit in front of the mic and play, and I recorded him directly to the two-track machine, thinking these were just demos. I gave him the unedited reels each time he left the session. Back then, editing involved using a razor blade, cutting the tape, and putting leader tape at the beginning and ending of songs if they were going to be used to manufacture records, commercial spots, and the like. I had learned to do this quite well but just gave him the full reel since, to my knowledge, these were for his use only. I learned later that Tom had been sending the reels off to a company called Rainbow Records, which would press up your reels into vinyl records. There is no telling how much money he spent doing that—and all with unedited songs, complete with some of his colorful comments in between takes.

All kinds of people came through the doors in those early years, but each experience taught me something and helped prepare me for the next opportunity, big or small.

Chapter 16

FIRST COMES LOVE

I hadn't seen Michelle in a while, besides running into her in the mall during the summer. Later in '87, I received a call from her, and she wanted to record some songs using accompaniment tracks as a Christmas present for her parents. She called on a Friday, and we got together the next Monday. We recorded Monday and Tuesday afternoon. I remember we'd go to the kitchen area there in the building on breaks and have cookies and cider, which were being served because it was Christmastime. Tuesday night, I suggested that we go eat dinner together. We went to a Chinese restaurant in town and had a really good time; it was obvious that we immediately clicked. I remember feeling so happy just being with her. She had what I would describe as a glowing countenance, and I loved everything about her.

During that week, we got together several times, and one day she brought homemade cookies to the studio, wrapped in foil with a red ribbon on top. We kept hanging out that December. We'd sit at the piano, and I'd sing and play for her, and she'd always want me to sing "just one more." I was impressed with her vocal ability as well; she had improved and matured since the first time I heard her. Her voice was crystal clear. I remember playing her Christmas recording for different people to hear, including my parents.

"I'm going to try and get her to date me," I told my mother as we were listening to the recording.

"I wouldn't get my hopes up on that. She's probably got more boyfriends than she knows what to do with," said my mother, ever the skeptic.

At some point after Christmas, Michelle and I discussed what she wanted to do with her music. She had wanted to sing Christian music since her early teens. I thought she had what it took to make it in the inspirational market at that time, and I felt she could have a career in it if that was what she wanted. She was a bit like Sandi Patty, with a more contemporary flair. She had completed a year and a half of studies at Shorter College in Rome, Georgia, a school known for its excellent music program. She had been chosen as Outstanding Freshman Music Student the year before, so she was already making her mark at Shorter. She was smart and obviously had a lot going for her. She did not, however, want to teach, as so many who major in music end up doing at some point, but wanted to be a performer.

We talked about her recording an album and seeing what would come of it. By this point, it was clear that my interest in Michelle was not "all business," and I was looking forward to working with her on a complete project and spending the time with her that I knew we would need to get the job done. She decided that she would take the dangerous "semester off" from school, from which so many never return, to work on the project. We worked on the album from January until April, and sometime during that period, I realized I just couldn't see myself ever being with anyone else.

Michelle was definitely different from other girls and didn't seem afraid or daunted by dating or being with someone with a disability. In fact, she said that she didn't see me as having a disability. She clearly saw me as someone who had to overcome some obstacles, but she seemed to respect me for the things I'd accomplished in my life so far. She always said that even though I couldn't see her the way others could, I saw her heart, and she very much liked that. We started to talk about the future because our friendship had definitely turned into something deeper. In May, around Michelle's birthday, I decided I was going to buy an engagement ring. I went to a local jeweler where my parents always bought their jewelry and purchased a modest solitaire. I kept it for a few days while I worked up my courage, even though we had talked about it, and she probably knew what was coming. When I decided it was time, I suggested that we go to a local park to walk around down by the lake. I had the idea to put the ring in a napkin in my shoe and pretend that something was wrong with my shoe and have her discover the ring. It seems kind of lame now, compared to the elaborate schemes people come up with to propose, but then it seemed sort of original and cute. After we'd walked around a bit, I bent down and fiddled with my shoe.

"I think there's something in my shoe," I said.

She bent down too to see what it was.

"Oh, I think I found it," I said as I smoothly pulled out the ring.

She giggled a little, but I don't think she was too surprised. She did say yes, and with our whole lives and future ahead of us at ages twenty-two and twenty, a wedding was planned for August. Back then, people typically had shorter engagements and married much earlier than they do today, so it was quick, but not all that out of the ordinary for it to be so. We did encounter some resistance from her parents, who were understandably concerned about Michelle marrying at such a young age and without having completed her education. They were also concerned about my ability to provide for her, and I understand all of this now as I look back on it, although it was very hurtful at the time.

Our ceremony and reception were held at First Baptist Church in Gainesville, and on August 27, 1988, we committed our lives, our abilities, and whatever we had to God and each other. It was the greatest day of my life to that point, only to be surpassed by the birth of my children in years to come. Part of our plan for the future included relocating to Nashville, Tennessee, where all roads eventually seem to lead if you are serious about being involved in the music business. Weeks before, we had made plans to move there, traveling up and finding an apartment and making all the necessary arrangements. After a short honeymoon trip to Sky Valley, one week after we were married, we made the move to Nashville, taking all our belongings in a Ryder truck and a Chevy Cavalier. We had rented a two-bedroom townhouse apartment for $325 a month. We loved married life and our new life in the big city and, in those new surroundings, got to settle into being a family and a couple all on our own.

One thing I knew I needed to do immediately was learn how to get around town on my own. When John Jarrard had lost his sight, he had some mobility training, and people were amazed at how he could navigate and get himself anywhere he needed to be on the streets of Nashville. I had never even attempted to use a cane before, so I knew this was going to be a big challenge in front of me. But I also knew I needed to have a better sense of navigation in the downtown area. If I were going to work and have a life in Nashville, I thought this was something essential. I went through the Services for the Blind and got on the schedule to begin mobility training. I started the training process in October with my instructor, Brenda Adams.

Brenda was in her midthirties with a Midwestern accent and a lot of patience. She was very good at what she did. We began our work at home around the apartment. I had to get used to the cane method—walk, tap—walk, tap—walk, tap. You have to do it in a certain rhythm, and it took some getting used to, but soon I was feeling ready to test my new skills on the street. We went to West End and the surrounding streets, onto Music Row, with Brenda beside me for assistance if needed. We went to the heart of downtown, where West End turns into Broadway, and some of the tricky one-way streets in that area.

Every Tuesday and Thursday morning at seven thirty, we would do this, rain or shine. It was very difficult at first, even with Brenda there to help; but little by little, she would decrease the amount of assistance she was giving me. Eventually, she would walk behind me or watch from a distance as I walked the streets on my own. Sometimes she would even follow in the car. We also worked on things like riding the city bus and going to places of interest around town. One place I remember going was Hickory Hollow Mall, a large shopping mall in the area. Brenda would explain to me the diagram of the mall and where certain shops were. Then she would say, "Okay, go find Dillard's," and I'd set off in that direction. We also went to the Nashville International Airport, and I learned to navigate around there. All of this did give me a feeling of independence but was quite nerve-wracking at the same time. It never really got to the point where I was not a bit nervous and apprehensive, but I did become more self-assured during the process.

Another immediate need for us was to find a good church to attend. We started visiting and then soon joined Two Rivers Baptist Church, a large church out near Opryland. As with nearly every big church in Nashville, there were a lot of professional musicians who attended and looked for ways to serve as they played in the church orchestras and bands. During this time, I was trying to get work as a session player and was not having too much luck. One opportunity I did have came from Tom Reeves, who owned a studio called Westpark Sound and who also played drums in the Two Rivers orchestra. I had joined the orchestra and was playing keyboards, so I got to know some of the other players. I struck up a friendship with Tom, and it wasn't long before he asked me to play overdubs on a session.

The day of the session, I don't know what happened, but it was a complete disaster. I can't say for sure if it was nerves or trying too hard, but I just couldn't deliver. It was a real disappointment and made me wonder if I was cut out for session work after all. Also at Two Rivers, I met up with a songwriter named Pam Andrews, who had just started to write children's musicals. She, Michelle, and I seemed to have an immediate connection, and I started demoing her songs. She became a good friend during our time in Nashville, and she did end up getting her first musical published, one that I had demoed in the small studio I had set up in our second bedroom. I would continue to work with her over the next couple of years, and she became a prolific writer of children's music.

While I struggled to find consistent work, Michelle had landed a job in the sales department at Brentwood Music, a record company in Brentwood, Tennessee. She called on Christian book and music stores and let them know about new products from Brentwood, a specialty company that sold children's music, choral music, and genre-specific instrumental music. Once, when the choral department at Brentwood realized they had left out a solo on one of the pieces on the demo choral tape for one of their collections, the producer got Michelle to come in and record the verse in the studio they had on site. Someone found out that she had done some recording and had just done an album, so they knew she could do it. She thought it might lead to other opportunities for her, but that was the only time she was asked to do anything like that at Brentwood.

Even though we loved our time in Nashville, we began to sense that the time was just not right to put down permanent roots. Michelle had done her album, but we really hadn't been where we could see what it would do, and I was also missing the opportunities I had become so accustomed to having in a place where I was fairly well known. We were feeling the nudge of what we sensed was God calling us back home—and possibly into a ministry of our own on a more full-time basis. We had begun to dig into the Scriptures in a new way for God's direction in our lives, and that lead to inspiration to write some new songs. After some prayer and consideration, we made an appointment to talk to the pastor who had married us, John Lee Taylor, about the possibility of returning and having First Baptist Church as our home base.

In those days, many churches had what were termed "staff music evangelists," nonpaid positions but designed to give the musician(s) a home base and support when they were not on the road. The musicians would be called upon to sing and participate in various things when they were not singing somewhere else. It was mutually beneficial for the church and the musicians. Dr. Taylor offered this to us, the title of staff music evangelists, as well as a small office on the church campus for our convenience. Sensing that this was the move we should make, we headed back to Gainesville a year after we had moved, not defeated but with a new sense of purpose and excitement.

Michelle and I were honestly just as excited to move back to Gainesville in 1989 as we had been to move to Nashville the previous year. We were glad to get to be with our families again following a time of being away and connecting as a couple. We were ready to dive into what we felt God calling us to do, melding our music with the faith that was central to our lives. It was good to have the support of First Baptist Church, but we knew we would need some things to make it possible for us to travel, one of which was a vehicle large enough to carry a sound system, luggage, and any merchandise we might have. We had a small two-door Chevy Cavalier at the time, and we needed more room than it could provide. We made an appointment to talk with a local car dealer in town, Milton Martin, who was known for helping people, especially with Christian-based ministries. We were hoping he might take the Cavalier on a trade and give us a good deal on a larger vehicle so our payments wouldn't be too high. We sat down in his office and talked. We talked about everything, not just cars. He talked about his son who was in ministry, and he wanted to hear all about what we were doing. He stopped me midsentence to make a phone call.

"Wait just a minute, I'm going to call somebody about you singing somewhere."

So he called and got us a gig right then and there. He was a real go-getter, and when an idea would strike him, he would act on it quickly. Following the phone call, I continued to fill him in on what we were doing and what our plans were—to travel and do youth camps, conferences, etc. Before I could even get to the point of asking for his help, he stopped me midsentence again.

"What can I do to help you? What do you need—a van, a station wagon, what?" he asked.

"We need something safe, large enough to haul sound equipment and get us from point A to point B," I said.

"Let's go out on the lot and see what we can find," he said.

We went outside, and he walked over to a slightly used Toyota minivan.

"I think this one will be really nice, just what you need," he said.

We looked inside the van, and it was perfect, but I assumed the price difference would be too great with what the small Cavalier would bring on a trade.

"Mr. Martin, this is so nice," I said. "But I don't think we will be able to afford anything like this."

"Well, if we're going to do it, we're going to do it first class! You have that car, don't you? I'll just take it on an even trade—you won't owe anything," he said without hesitation.

Michelle and I were both flabbergasted, overwhelmed, and couldn't believe that someone could be so kind and generous. We drove the van off the lot that day, thankful for an answered prayer and thankful for the one through whom it was answered.

All the pieces seemed to be falling into place, and we began to focus in earnest on getting ready for performances and pulling together promotional materials to send to churches and other venues. Support with donations of money or services seemed to come just when we needed them to accomplish the next step. We officially set up our ministry and called on some well-respected leaders and old friends to be on our board of directors. After pulling all this together, we did a "kickoff" concert at First Baptist Church on a Sunday evening in early October. Family and friends were there, and we sang to a packed house that night. One of our new board members, Frank Henry, along with Milton Martin, had been in California for a Toyota show and flew back a day early just to be at the concert. Frank Henry was working fairly closely with us at this time and knew we were trying to put the funds together for a duet album of some of the new material we had recently written. He and Mr. Martin had evidently discussed this on the flight home because after the concert, Milton Martin came up and requested us to come see him that week.

"I want you to come to my office on Tuesday and let's talk about something," he said.

We didn't know what it was about, but of course complied with the request. We sat down in his office on Tuesday morning, and without too much preamble, he began, "This album you want to do, how much is it going to cost to do it?"

I had recently explored the possibility with Tom Reeves about recording a project at Westpark Sound, with him helping to produce it with me. I had a quote from him of $14,200 for the whole project, which at that time sounded like $14 million to me. I explained to Mr. Martin about the proposal and told him the amount.

"Well, you can tell him you've got the money. I'll write a commitment letter telling him to go ahead with it," he said matter-of-factly.

The generosity of this man was an unbelievable blessing, and it allowed us to be able to do all the things we did during this period in our lives and ministry.

Recording the album was a dream come true. We had the opportunity to use some of the best studio musicians in the business, an all-star cast, and form some relationships that would last through the years. One of those was with a guitar player named Tom Hemby. Tom Hemby knew Tom Reeves because they had both been in the well-known group the Imperials together. Tom's wife, Deana, was personal assistant to Amy Grant. I was in awe of Tom's ability on guitar. He would go on to produce, tour, or write with many big-name artists, both secular and Christian, such as Faith Hill, Wynonna Judd, Kenny Loggins, Michael McDonald, Amy Grant, Donna Summer, Vince Gill, Ricky Skaggs, Steven Curtis Chapman, and the list goes on and on. Tom also produced the multi-artist soundtrack for Mel Gibson's *Passion of the Christ*. Tom played on half of the tracks for the album, and the other half of the guitar tracks were played by Mark Baldwin, whose credits include Whitney Houston, Stevie Wonder, Aretha Franklin, Steven Curtis Chapman, Natalie Grant, and many others. Tom Reeves played drums, as well as wearing the producer hat. Tom had played with the Imperials for many years and managed Westpark Creative Group.

On bass, we had Craig Nelson, who was also one of the sought-after studio musicians and played on all the top Christian records of the day. Ted Wilson held down the keyboard spot, and I did all the keyboard overdubs, all my nervousness gone compared to my last experience with keyboard overdubs at Westpark Sound. Doing background vocals were Dave Holloway, Chris Rodriguez, and myself. Dave was a friend from Two Rivers and sang background vocals on many Christian records at that time. Chris was an amazing vocalist who would end up having a varied and interesting career, doing everything from playing guitar and singing background vocals for big-name artists, to being director of A & R and the president of various record companies through the years. Chris most recently was on tour playing guitar with such artists as Kelly Clarkson, Keith Urban, and Faith Hill. It was from Chris that I learned that eating potato chips could help you hit the high notes. I remember the three of us standing at the mic, and Chris's voice was so powerful that he kept having to back up and soon was standing against the wall in the vocal booth. We had Chris singing the high part.

"Man, how can we get those high notes like you do?" asked Dave Holloway.

"Potato chips, man," was Chris's answer.

I guess it's something about the grease in the chips, but not really sure why it seems to work.

"Okay, chip up," Chris would say, and we'd all eat a chip in between takes.

In some circles, it's drugs and alcohol in the studio; but in our case, the worst thing we put in our bodies was potato chips. We were all young and skinny then, so we didn't have to worry about calories. We did come up with some unbelievable background vocals that day.

It took a few months to complete the album, with Michelle and me traveling back and forth and staying in Econo Lodges and Red Roof Inns to try and save on expenses. We were pleased with the result and had a product that we could put in people's hands and sell to help support ourselves.

We were staying quite busy singing at various events, conferences, camps, and churches. We traveled all over, sometimes flying, but most of the time driving our blue Toyota minivan, which was a dependable vehicle for years. It got us everywhere we needed to go, from Virginia to Florida and places in between. Things were fast-paced, but even so, there was downtime, especially during the week. I began to think about getting my own studio equipment back up and running and making use of it. It had been dismantled and stored, and it was a mess. I knew it would take some doing to get it functioning again. Many things would have to be soldered together, and everything would have to be moved back into place. I got permission to use my old space again and decided to begin the rebuilding process. I enlisted the help of Dale Woody, one of the sound people at First Baptist Church. He worked with me for about a week, making sense of everything and putting humpty dumpty back together again. When it was done, there was immediate interest in the studio, and I did my first session in it the Friday after it was completed. So we entered into an even busier season, with me doing demos and production like I had done in the past in addition to our travel schedule.

One of the people Michelle and I had the occasion to meet during this time was Babbie Mason. She is a prolific singer/songwriter and was in the height of her career at that point. She was based in Atlanta, and in 1990, Michelle and I met with her at her offices. She gave us advice and wisdom about music ministry in general and encouraged us in what we were doing. It was the beginning of a long and enduring friendship with Babbie, as well as her husband, Charles. During those years, Babbie held retreats for aspiring song-writers and artists, which Michelle and I attended as participants in 1990. The next year, she asked me to lead one of the seminars about the recording process. I did and continued to teach at her seminars for several years.

During the early '90s, I had the opportunity to work with many interesting people in the studio. One of those was a lady named Penny Waddell, who wrote children's musicals. I did all of Penny's demos. I charged $125 per demo, and it would take me forever to complete one. Through Penny, I got to know people in a group called Trinity. I did an original song for them, and they determined that they wanted me to produce a full album for them. They had a large budget, so it was decided that we would record in Nashville since the budget would allow. It was my first experience actually producing a project for someone else in Nashville with studio musicians. It took us a few months to complete it, and I really enjoyed the production process and once again being surrounded by such excellent musicians in the studio.

Chapter 17

OLYMPIC-SIZED DREAMS

In the summer of 1990, Atlanta was chosen to host the '96 Olympics. It was an even bigger honor because it was the centennial anniversary of Olympic Games. The announcement came from Tokyo, Japan, early in the morning, and we were up long before dawn to watch the special coverage of the event. For months, there had been a lot of hype about Atlanta being one of the six cities in the running, and everyone was on pins and needles to hear if we were going to be chosen. People had packed areas all around Atlanta just waiting for the announcement. It was an exciting time to be living in North Georgia. The rowing and equestrian venues were to be held in and around Gainesville, so it would mean a lot for our city as well. I still remember the announcement in the thick accent of the president of the International Olympic Committee.

"The International Olympic Committee has awarded the 1996 Olympic Games to the city of—Atlanta!"

Dignitaries and former mayors, including Maynard Jackson, whom I had met and lunched with so many years earlier, were in Japan as a part of the delegation from Atlanta. There was much excitement and rejoicing here and in Japan when the announcement was made. I decided that day that I wanted to write an Olympic-themed song in hopes that it might be used in some way throughout the games. I didn't have any idea how I might get it in the right hands to be used or even what the song would be at that point. The evening of the announcement, Michelle and I went with Penny Waddell and her husband, Bill, to a songwriter's event. I told Penny about my idea, and she jumped right on it, offering to help me do whatever needed to be done. Bill and Penny knew a lot of people, and she was the type of persistent person who would find something out if she didn't know. In those days, you either got on the phone or had to go visit somebody to get things done. At that time, she had two little girls at home and had just found out they were expecting baby number three, so she had her hands full.

Michelle and I immediately set to work writing. It didn't take us long to come up with the song, which we titled "Follow the Dream." It was one of those that just seemed to write itself:

Chorus
Follow the dream
Shoot for your star
This time it's real
You've made it this far
The hope that you bring
The best you can be
This is your chance
To let the world see
So follow the dream

I demoed it, playing all the instruments myself and singing it. I used a group of children on the last chorus to give it a youthful, hopeful feel. We were pleased with the song, and it seemed to get everyone's approval that heard it. Through Penny's efforts, contact was made with the offices of Billy Payne, head of the Atlanta Olympic Committee, which had been dubbed the "dream team." It was a long process, but after months of trying, she finally found the right person in his office to talk to, and the song worked its way up through the ranks. It made it into the top 5 selections from local songwriters that would go up against national and international submissions to be the theme song for the Olympic Games. We were beyond excited but knew it was still a long shot.

In 1995, we got word that David Foster's "The Power of the Dream" had been chosen and that Celine Dion would record it and perform the song at the opening ceremonies. David Foster is one of my biggest musical influences, especially as a producer. He's still on the top 10 list of people I'd like to meet, so it was an honor for my song to get beaten out by something he had written! About the same time, though, I was contacted by the Olympic offices to go on a mini "goodwill" tour to Japan, along with some other Georgia musicians, but something was to happen in October that would be much more exciting and would prevent me from participating in the tour.

Back to 1990, the studio was busy, but we were continuing to travel and sing, and with the holidays always came even more opportunities. Michelle and I sang for a Christmas Tree lighting for the town of Lawrenceville that year, and one person in attendance was someone I would end up working closely with for several years, Ron Baker. Ron was an unbelievable musician and songwriter and had recently started playing with another talented guitar player, Bob Lehman. They called themselves *Ron Baker and Bob*. Ron and Bob had just begun to sing at some local events and churches and wanted to record an album. Ron came up to me after we sang, and we talked for a while. He found out I had a studio and was interested in exploring the possibility of me recording a project for him. I sent Ron home with a copy of our album, but it was a few months before I heard from Ron again, and he scheduled a time for him and Bob to come to Gainesville. They were both impressed with the album I had given to Ron.

"You've got a lot going on, on the album—a lot of texture that we really like. We want you to produce our album," Ron told me when we finally met again.

I was excited to have the opportunity to work with them. One thing that Ron wanted was for Babbie Mason to come sing background vocals and adlib some vocals on the end of one song. We called Babbie, and she agreed to come and sing. There was never any pretention with Babbie; she was always willing to help. The daughter and sister of a whole passel of preachers, she was the real deal and was more concerned with forming relationships and reaching people than any kind of fame or status, even though she had both. She, Michelle, and I did the three-part harmony for the background vocals, and then she put the most amazing stuff on the end of the song in typical Babbie style. It was awesome and really took the song called "Lift Him Up" to a new level. The song began to get some radio play on the Christian station that served the greater Atlanta area, 91.5 FM. The station very seldom played "independent" artists, but I think with Babbie Mason being on the title track, they decided to add it into the rotation. This helped propel Ron and Bob to a new level and brought about many opportunities for them.

The year 1991 was busy. We built our first house, and it was exciting to be able to take this next step after having been apartment dwellers for several years. Christmas again rolled around quickly. One distinct honor we had that year was to sing at the Christian Financial Concepts Christmas banquet. Christian Financial Concepts was an organization founded by Larry Burkett, whom many will remember as the first financial "guru" to teach biblical precepts about money. Larry was a nationally known bestselling author, and people followed his advice like they do Dave Ramsey today. We had also written a Christmas song that year called "Mary's Song." It was being played on several radio stations in the area. We sang it everywhere and were even interviewed by one of the stations which had played it during the season, WDUN, on Christmas Eve morning. It was through that program that another important musical connection was made for me. The father of Rick Pruitt just happened to be listening to WDUN that morning and wrote down my contact information. He told Rick later that day, "I have a Christmas present for you." It was my phone number.

Chapter 18

Movin' On Up

Rick Pruett called shortly after the new year began and explained to me how his dad had given him my number. Rick had done some recording in the past with his musical partner and friend Mark Davis. Mark lived in Cincinnati, and the two of them hadn't worked together in about ten years. Plans were made for the recording to take place, and Mark came down to Georgia for several days in February. Rick and Mark played these oversized acoustic guitars, and their sound was phenomenal. The very first day I was to record them and was getting the mics set up, I kept hearing a ticking sound. I thought maybe one of them had a loud watch on, but it was an unusual rhythm for a watch.

"Whose watch is ticking?" I asked from the control room over the talkback.

Rick kind of laughed and explained that he had an artificial heart valve, and that's what I was hearing. Rick was in his late thirties, but as a young man in his twenties, Rick had undergone the valve replacement for a congenital heart defect. Rick was healthy and active and had even become a vegetarian to try and take care of his heart. It was always a challenge to try and mask that ticking on the recordings because the microphones were so sensitive, and Rick's songs had a lot of dynamic changes with soft passages in them. Our running joke became that all of Rick and Mark's songs should be the tempo of Rick's heart, and Rick should try not to get his heart rate elevated during takes. It was the beginning of a long, enduring relationship as we would work together for the next seven years.

We had just come through a very busy summer in 1992, and one morning in August, I walked into the studio to fire it up for the day. The building was huge, and I would enter at the far end of it and walk some distance back to the area where the studio was. I unlocked the door to my control room to find that there was standing water in it that poured out when I opened the door. I remember the sinking, helpless, hopeless feeling of just not knowing what to do. I ran back to the other end of the building to see if I could catch Michelle before she drove off. I was able to flag her down, and we immediately went to work pulling things out, getting things off the floor, and trying to salvage anything we could. We would later find out that the landscape people had left a soaking hose going, and there was no runoff for it, so it just backed up into the building. My studio doors at the bottom were sealed so well for soundproofing purposes that water had not been able to flow through a crack in the door, and the water was simply held in those two rooms, almost as if they had been sealed. Miraculously, though, some things were damp, but nothing was permanently damaged or destroyed because of the water.

Following the flood, we knew we had to find someplace to move and set up shop. There had been recent talk of plans to tear the building down to build a new, bigger bank building in the same location. Now that it had flooded, there was no way Home Federal was going to pay for it to be cleaned up when they had plans to tear it down soon. We began to look around town for other spaces we might rent, contemplating the leap of faith and what it would mean to our future. We saw a space for rent in the local newspaper on Northside Drive in the heart of downtown Gainesville and made arrangements with the owner to go look at the space. It was in an older strip building, with an attorney's office at one end and a shoe repair shop at the other. There were two empty spaces for rent side by side next to the shoe-repair shop. Our thought all along was to expand if we were going to move into a new space. One of the spaces would have only been about the same amount of space I had in the bank building. We determined that we could knock down a wall and combine the two spaces, giving us ample room in the control room and live room, in addition to an office space and lobby area. We really wanted the space but needed to weigh the options and not jump into something we couldn't handle.

In the bank building, we had not had to pay rent or utilities, so this was going to be a big step. We went to talk to some of our good friends Jack and Carole (CJ) Wehmiller and get their guidance about what we should do next. Jack worked for Kemper Financial and traveled all over the world selling Kemper products. CJ was the pastor's secretary at First Baptist Church. We were about twenty years younger than they and had valued their advice and wisdom through the years. We had some good times with them, Jack usually keeping us in stiches with his humor and stories of the road. We initially met Jack and CJ through First Baptist Church when they had not lived in Gainesville for very long. We still had an office at First Baptist Church and would see CJ more frequently. There were several times Michelle would see Jack in or around CJ's office, invariably teasing someone or telling a joke. She had no idea what he did for a living at that time but began to feel sorry for CJ, thinking Jack didn't have a job and maybe couldn't even get one because he was such a jokester. Little did she know, Jack was making more money than he probably knew what to do with and had some downtime in between his trips, which was why he would be in the church offices from time to time. They had moved to Gainesville because it was far enough from the hustle and bustle of Atlanta but close enough for Jack to get to the airport fairly quickly. Later on in our friendship, Michelle told Jack of her initial impression of him, and I don't think I had heard him ever laugh as hard as he did at that. He told Michelle that she had him pegged right: he was hanging out in CJ's office on payday, waiting for her to get her check so he could spend the grocery money on beer! We still get a good laugh out of that sometimes when we get together. It was one of those life lessons where you learn things are not always as they appear!

At that time, Jack and CJ lived in town but had purchased a large amount of land out in the country, which they were going to build their dream house on. They went through a phase where they wanted to live on a farm, so they were going to put a barn on the property. Jack said, "Well, if nothing else, you can put the studio in the barn and call it 'Barn to Lose.'" We decided against that, but I do remember something else Jack said that night. He said, "Someday you're going to be in a place where that amount you're having to pay for rent is going to seem small and insignificant compared to what the space is going to do for you." So after prayer, consideration, and counsel from friends and family, we decided to take the next logical step and go into business "for real." We took out a small loan and began the process of converting the two spaces into one. It required cutting a hole in a firewall for a window between the control room and live room, as well as a door between the rooms. Several specialized things had to be done to make it studio-ready, and it took a couple of months for it to be completed.

During the downtime, I received a call from a lady named Pat Thomson. She was from Tifton, a small town in South Georgia, and had been given my name by a girl who had interned with me as a part of Brenau College's Summer Spark program. Pat initially told me about her connection to Alan Jackson, having taught his wife in Sunday school when she was a child. Then she told me about her daughter Cyndi, who was fifteen years old and was an aspiring country singer. Back then, it was unusual for an artist that young to try and break into the music business, unlike today where they seemed to start younger and younger. Pat wanted Cyndi to do some demos of cover tunes just to see how she sounded and to give her some experience with recording. I explained to Pat that we were under construction with the new studio but would be up and running soon. We ended up scheduling the time, and Cyndi Thomson was my first session in the new space. We didn't even have things completely finished, but all the equipment was set up, and we were able to start working. Cyndi would come in and out of the studio, and our lives, over the next five years or so. I knew from the first day I heard her that she had what it took to make it and would even say so in a newspaper article that was written about the opening of the studio. My remarks in the paper about Cyndi's ability and future turned out to be prophetic.

I had also lined up another project with a promising artist, Karen Moore, during our time of being under construction. So business resumed with a couple of good projects, and I felt encouraged that we were, in fact, going to be able to make a go of it in the new space. After I finished Cyndi's and Karen's projects, I heard from Ron Baker again. Ron and Bob were still enjoying success with their first project, "Lift Him Up," and wanted to be able to follow it up with something that would surpass the first album. After some discussion about the project and expectations for it, plans were made for production to begin. Before starting Ron's project, though, Cyndi Thomson booked some more studio time and wanted to record original songs. I called on my old friends Bruce Birch and John Jarrard for some original material. We recorded one of Bruce's songs called "Leave Him to Me" and one of John's called "Hooked Again." I continued to be impressed with Cyndi's ability and knew it was just a matter of time before she got discovered and picked up by a major label.

Not long after the studio opened, I acquired the invaluable help of a second engineer. John Broaddus had seen the studio and walked in off the street one day to talk to me. He was interested in the recording process and offered his services just to be able to learn more about it. John was in his early forties and had made some money in real estate. He had several rental properties he managed but had a good deal of time day to day to pursue other things he enjoyed. I taught him about recording, but he ended up being a big help to me as well, and I appreciated his friendship.

The first big project John helped me on was the Ron Baker project. I knew immediately that this was going to be a very different project. As is often the case with a second project, there seemed to be a lot of tension and pressure to create something better than we'd done on the previous album. Ron had written some great material, and we did have some fun times during the recording process, but things were so strained that after a few months, the project just fell apart and would lay dormant for some twenty years.

The year went on with some smaller projects, songwriter demos, and such, which saw us through; and in the summer, I received a call from my mentor and friend Byron Cutrer. Byron was still minister of student music at First Baptist Church Orlando at that time and was in a prolific time of songwriting. He was writing musicals, and a patriotic musical he had written had just been published. He had some original songs for an upcoming musical that he wanted me to work on. I had a great time reconnecting, and he would come back at the end of the year again to work on some songs for a Christmas musical.

Also in 1993, Rick Pruett and Mark Davis had just signed with a small jazz label called Rising Star Records. Rick and Mark had played at the Montreux Jazz Festival that summer and had the inspiration to do their next project. They had written some new material; plus, we recut some of the songs they had done on their first album. John Broaddus and I worked together on the album titled *Breaking the Rules*. It was a great record, and I particularly enjoyed working on it. The project even received a Grammy nomination, which as the engineer, included me as well!

Chapter 19

Little 3

The studio was quite busy on into 1994, so the natural progression was to back off on our concert/singing schedule. We also transitioned to a church where Michelle's extended family had been members all of her life. It was a large and growing church, and we had wondered for some time if we might be more useful in that setting than where we were. One Sunday, we decided to visit Blackshear Place and sit in the balcony, hoping to be able to observe their services without being noticed. We thought we were under the radar, but it turned out we had been seen by quite a few people; and the next morning, Don Gibson, the minister of music at Blackshear Place Baptist Church, called to tell me he was glad to have us in the service and asked if we would be willing to come down and sing in their service in a couple of weeks.

The Sunday that we were there was the first Sunday in a new building for them, and there was a great sense of purpose and excitement in the place. We immediately felt right at home and loved the music. We did go and sing there a couple of weeks later and really had the sense that it was time for us to move into another phase in our life and ministry. In some ways, it was difficult to leave First Baptist, but we felt like it was the right decision at the time. Blackshear Place was about two miles from our new house, and there we formed many friendships with people who became an integral part of our lives, sharing the ups and downs that young families experience in that phase of life.

We were young, in our sixth year of marriage, and just beginning to think about starting a family. When Michelle and I thought about having a baby, it was not without some reservation, given the fact the real cause of my blindness was unknown. Dr. Michael Connor, Michelle's doctor, said he was almost certain that my condition did not have genetic basis but was caused by something that happened in utero while my mother was carrying me. This was reassuring, but still there was a tremendous amount of faith involved in starting our family. Not faith that everything would turn out exactly as we wanted it—although, of course, we hoped and prayed for a healthy baby in every respect—but the faith that God would see us through and be with us, whatever we had to face.

We also realized that every pregnancy involves the unknown, and prospective parents are always concerned that their baby will be healthy and whole. In February of 1995, we found out we were expecting our first baby and were excited to be entering this new phase in our lives. I remember the day well that Michelle had taken a pregnancy test and called me at work with the news. I was so excited and distracted that I made quite a few blunders that day. I had to talk with someone at Word Records that afternoon about an upcoming trip to Nashville, and I responded to one of her questions with something that I realized made no sense whatsoever once it was out of my mouth.

"I'm sorry, we just found out we're going to have a baby, and I'm very distracted right now!" I said apologetically.

She laughed and chalked up my gaff to the pregnancy news. As I prepared for the trip, I really didn't want to leave Michelle. People were just beginning to get cell phones, and I had had one for some time. I made sure before I left that she had a cell phone too, just for security's sake. The day of the trip, there were awful storms in the area, and I felt very apprehensive about flying. It was like I had a whole new perspective, realizing that another life was going to be dependent on me. It was a rough flight, but I did make it there and back without incident.

We were anxious to find out if our baby was a boy or girl and made an appointment to go to a place called Fetal Fotos to have an ultrasound video when Michelle was about eighteen weeks along. We were so excited, and again I was unable to focus on anything else. I had worn some khaki pants and a button-down shirt to our appointment, along with some dress shoes, two *different* dress shoes. They were similar in style but different shades of brown. Michelle hadn't noticed it either before we left the house, but started giggling while we were in the Fetal Fotos lobby waiting to go back, and I had one leg propped up on the other knee.

"What is it?" I asked.

"You have on two different shoes," she whispered, trying to contain herself.

"Oh my gosh, I do!" I said, surprised.

Just then, the ultrasound technician called, "Mr. and Mrs. Dowdy."

Michelle got all settled, and the technician began looking at the eighteen-week-old life residing safe inside its mother. She pointed out a "nice spine," a foot, legs, fluttering heart, brain, and pronounced that everything looked good. Even though it was not meant to be a diagnostic session, the technician was certified and had many years of experience doing ultrasound in an OB/GYN office, so it was reassurance that everything was forming as it should. During the video recording, she kept trying to get a peek to determine what sex the baby was. Just when she thought she could see, the baby would move, almost as if it were playing hide-and-seek and didn't want us to know. She went back and forth on what sex she thought the baby was but had not gotten that view that she wanted to be 100 percent certain. Our session was drawing to a close, and she gave it one last try.

"I've got it…there it is!" She paused for suspense before finally saying, "Mark, you have a son. There's your boy, right there." She pointed to the region she could now see clearly that confirmed *boy*.

I, of course, could not really see any of this in detail, only that there was a screen in close proximity. We were excited. It was nice to be able to start thinking of a real little person in terms of being a boy. We had fun thinking about names. Up until that point, we had referred to him as "little 3" since he made us a family of three. We finally decided on the first name of Graham, after evangelist Billy

Graham, but were undecided on a middle name. We had seen Dr. Graham when he had done a crusade in Atlanta in 1994 and were amazed at the response of the people in the Georgia Dome. What better heritage could he have, we asked ourselves, than to be named for such a man?

About this same time was when I received the invitation to go to Japan in October as one of several local musicians to build "good will" for the Olympic Games. I was honored, but the baby's due date was October 9, and I was not going to miss it for anything. The pregnancy went along fine until about month six, when Michelle started experiencing a significant amount of swelling. It was hot that summer, one of the hottest on record and certainly the hottest in recent memory. The nurses at her doctor's office tried to reassure her.

"Honey, don't worry, it's so hot. Everybody's swelling," they'd say.

However, Michelle was beginning to develop high blood pressure and was headed toward preeclampsia, a condition that can be serious for both mother and baby. On August 13, Michelle told me she thought something was not right and that we should go to the hospital. Our fears were confirmed when the doctor told us Michelle was trying to go into preterm labor. They admitted her to the hospital, and it was hoped that with complete bed rest and other medical intervention, they might hold off the labor. If born then, Graham would be nearly eight weeks early. The doctor on call, not Michelle's regular doctor but in the same practice, painted a fairly grim picture.

"If he's born now, he'll be on a ventilator because his lungs are not developed yet," he said seriously.

They had apparently done a test that had revealed Graham's lungs were not developed enough yet to breathe on his own outside the womb. I remember the helpless feeling and praying silently as the doctor spoke.

"Lord, without you, without the Unseen Hand, we can't make it. We need *you* to intervene."

I did not stay with Michelle in the hospital that night; she was getting some specialized care and was attended by one nurse all night long. I left with an anxious heart but knowing they would call if anything started to happen. I stayed at my parents' house, which is not more than five minutes from the hospital. Immediately, we began to let family and friends know of the situation and requested prayer for Michelle and the baby. Michelle shared with me later about that night in the hospital. She did not sleep but was perfectly at peace. She said it was almost as if someone were literally holding her in their arms. She felt it was God's presence, or angels, with her that night, and she could also sense the prayers of many being lifted up for her and the baby.

That night passed uneventfully, and we thought that we might be in the hospital for quite some time. She was moved to a regular room since it looked like the danger had passed. The next night, however, Michelle began to experience what she felt were contractions. The nurses hooked her up to a machine with a belt that measured contractions and declared that she was not in labor. She was by herself, except for calling the nurses in every so often to tell them she thought she had to be in labor. They kept checking the machine, each time telling Michelle she was not having contractions. By morning, Michelle was still in distress.

"We'll have Dr. Dillard come in and take a look before she leaves, but I don't think you're in labor. She's been here all night delivering babies," offered one of the nurses.

Dr. Dillard came in and examined Michelle, who was by this time fully dilated. She had, in fact, labored all night, alone, with no pain medication or help of any kind. The machine had malfunctioned, we learned later. Dr. Dillard was alarmed and started barking out instructions.

"We're having a baby. Get on the phone to Egleston and get the angel team on the way up here. Come on, let's move!" she said urgently.

Michelle asked if she could have an epidural, which she had planned on.

"No, dear, it's much too late for that. You've done the hard part already. This baby's going to be here in just a few minutes," said Dr. Dillard.

They rushed Michelle into the delivery room on a stretcher. I was just sitting down at the kitchen table to eat a bowl of cereal, and the phone rang.

"This is Lisa from Northeast Georgia Medical Center. Can I speak to Mark Dowdy?" said the nurse on the other end of the line.

"This is Mark," I said.

"We're having a baby, and if you'd like to join in, you'd better get here quick," said Lisa in an excited tone.

My parents and I rushed to the hospital. A nurse was waiting for me outside the delivery room area with scrubs, a mask, and paper shoes to don before going into the room. In our haste, we accidentally went into the wrong room but soon found the right one. Michelle was just being instructed to "push" and was trying but exhausted from the night of labor. The stretcher she was on wouldn't lock, and every time she would push, it would move. Soon it was close enough to the door on the other side of the room that when said door was opened by pediatrician Mike Hosford, it banged into the stretcher. He was there to whisk the baby away as soon as he was born. There were some lighter moments such as those, but I was in a state of nonstop prayer (silent prayer—you don't want to scare your medical team) the entire time. I was scared for our baby named Graham, and I remember thinking, *This can't be happening*, but it was happening, and I kept praying, *God, You've got this. You've got this!*

"Come on, one good push," Dr. Dillard encouraged.

All of a sudden, there he was—his little head was out, and he started to cry, even before the rest of his body was delivered. We thought it was a good sign because it sounded like a hearty cry. It was a surreal moment. I felt like time had stopped, and I felt the Holy Spirit sweep into the room. There was that new life, that new soul, fresh from heaven. They examined him, and he looked good, but they whisked him away anyway. Immediately a nasal cannula with oxygen was placed on him, but he kept knocking it off. The angel team from Egleston Children's Hospital arrived shortly. At that time, our local hospital did not have a neonatal intensive care unit (NICU), and all babies that required specialized care had to go to Atlanta to Egleston. There was a special group of medical professionals called the *angel team* who would come and assess children and take them in the specialized ambulance back to Atlanta if need be.

When they arrived to examine Graham, to our surprise, they said they did not need to take him to Atlanta. He kept knocking the oxygen off, and they noticed that he was maintaining his oxygen saturation levels without the extra oxygen, so they just left it off from that point on. His lungs were, in fact, developed—no ventilator needed, a real answer to prayer. The only real difficulty he would have would be apnea, common in preemies, where he would "forget" to breathe. He was put on a monitor to detect these episodes, which sometimes occurred several times a day. It was nerve-wracking to hear the monitor go off, the signal that Graham was not breathing. But all that was required to get him going again was a little shake, or picking him up, and he was okay.

After a couple of days, Michelle was discharged from the hospital. It was hard leaving Graham there, but we were hopeful he would be home with us soon. He made a little progress each day but couldn't seem to gain weight. He needed to surpass his birth weight—four pounds, six ounce—in order to go home. We went each day to the nursery and held him for hours. On the twenty-fourth day after he was born, weighing just four pounds, nine ounces, Graham was able to come home from the hospital. He was still on the monitor, the leads attached to his chest with a tiny band to hold them in place. His diapers were so small; they looked like the rectangular napkins you get at a cheap burger joint. The day we finally got him home, we sat up really late, just holding him and taking it all in. The thing we had been the most concerned with, Graham's eyes, seemed to be 100 percent perfect.

It was amazing how a little person weighing less than a bag of sugar could so totally turn our lives upside down, but he did. We experienced that deep and intense love that most all parents have for their children. Michelle was, of course, consumed with Graham's care and his health and worried endlessly about the apnea, to the point of it being unhealthy for her. In those first couple of weeks Graham was home from the hospital, she began to be afraid to be left alone with him, fearful that he would suffer one of the apneic episodes, and she would not be able to revive him. Before leaving the hospital, we were required to go through an infant CPR course, which Michelle seemed to dwell on continually. She had anxiety to the point that she didn't want me to return to work. She cared for Graham as diligently as any mother ever has but was more at ease as long as someone was with her. I needed to get back to work, and not knowing what to do for her, I called our pediatrician Dr. Mike Hosford to see if he could give me any counsel as to how best to help Michelle get through this time. I told him of her fears, and I asked for his help with near desperation.

"Tell me, what can I do to help her?"

He was an older doctor, with years and years of wisdom and clinical experience, a beloved physician in our community.

"Well, you can tell her I've never lost a baby on a monitor. And tell her to trust God, and I'm not Him," he said in his typical straightforward manner.

I think that advice helped Michelle almost more than anything else could have, and we've recalled it many times through the years. While Michelle had been carrying Graham, even before the ultrasound that revealed his sex, she had a dream one night of a little boy. This little boy of about three to four years old in her dream stood at the end of the hall in our first home, grinning with his hands on his hips. She described him as having blond hair and blue eyes and wearing a white T-shirt and navy shorts. The image was very clear in her mind, although he looked different from the way her mind's eye had imagined a child of ours to look, expecting any child we had to have dark hair like mine. She knew immediately when she woke up that she had dreamed about the child she was carrying and assumed it was a vision from God that was given to her. When our fair-haired boy was born, it was further confirmation that this was the child in the dream. Later, this would sustain her and get her through some tough times of wondering if Graham would make it through infancy since she had seen him as a three- to four-year-old in her dream.

Even with the confidence the dream had given her, there were moments of doubt, particularly when the monitor would go off in the middle of the night as it was set to go off after several seconds with no detected breaths. Usually, the monitor sounding was due to Graham's movement and dislodging one of the leads. However, we would never know if it were going to be a true apneic episode as we rushed, hearts pounding, into the nursery, always afraid of what we would find. It was a nerve-wracking couple of months, but Graham's last apneic episode was on his due date, and he never, to our knowledge, had another one, although he continued to be on the monitor at night for some time to come. He did gain weight after we finally got him home, 2.6 pounds in the first month, to be exact.

We barely felt out of the woods with the apnea situation when Graham became very sick with RSV, a serious respiratory virus to which preemies are particularly susceptible. We spent our first Thanksgiving with Graham in the hospital. At night, Michelle would either sleep with him in the hospital bed under the oxygen tent, or we curled up together on the small couch. We spent a week in the hospital around the clock but were thankful that Graham could receive such excellent care. Through all this, we learned to trust God in new areas, believing that He had us in the palm of His hand.

Chapter 20

STUDIO DAZE

The first year with Graham was full of ups and downs, but we were finally settling into life with a new member of the family. It was summer of 1996, and the long-awaited Olympics were finally in Atlanta. The Olympic Torch came through Gainesville in front of Brenau University, and we were there to witness it. Graham was there too since we wanted to be able to tell him one day that he had been a part of the torch coming through our town, even though he would never remember it. I went to several of the Olympic events with some of Michelle's cousins, who were young and always up for lots of activity. It gave me an eerie feeling that I had been in Centennial Olympic Park the night before the bombing of it.

Around that time, I received a call from Babbie Mason. She had been invited to sing at a conference where Margaret Thatcher was to be the keynote speaker. They wanted her to sing the national anthem, and she needed a different arrangement of it and wanted to know if I would come up with an arrangement and record an accompaniment track for her. I was thrilled and honored and got to work on it right away.

Also, Rick Pruett came back into the studio to record a second album and had, by this time, added a couple of new members, making it the Pruett-Davis Quartet. It was a much more difficult process than it had been the first time when it had been just Rick and Mark. There were personalities, egos, and differences of opinion that sometimes got in the way of accomplishing the tasks at hand. The album would not be finished until 1997. Rick and Mark lost their deal with

Rising Star Records due to the process taking so long and ultimately had to fund the completion of it themselves.

In fall of 1996, which had been a slower year than usual business-wise, I was approached by an orthopedic surgeon that I knew about him becoming a partner in the business. He and his wife had an interest in the music business and were looking for a new project they could dive into. His wife, in particular, was going to be involved in the day-to-day running of the office. Michelle had run the office before Graham was born but had since gone back to school when Graham was only six months old, pursuing a degree in occupational therapy from Brenau University. So plans were made for our partnership, for some much-needed upgrades to equipment, and a name change to Crosstown Sound. My new partners were going to put in a sizeable sum to buy into the business, and with those funds, we were able to make the needed upgrades in addition to buying a midi-grand Yamaha piano, which I hand-picked myself during a trip to Nashville. The year 1997 brought several new and exciting projects, each one coming into view as the current one was wrapping up. I worked with Babbie Mason on a project for an artist she was producing, Debbie Nagel, the entire project being done at Crosstown Sound.

One of the most memorable artists I ever worked with was a guitarist named Fernando Aragon, who had played guitar with Carlos Santana for several years. He had heard about me from a drummer, Shannon Kori, I had worked with in the studio previously and contacted me about recording an album for him. Fernando was an amazing musician, and I enjoyed working on that project as well as playing some live shows with him.

Another exciting opportunity came when I attended a men's prayer breakfast for which Atlanta Braves first baseman Sid Bream was the keynote speaker. Sid was the one who made the famous slide into home plate, clinching the division title for the Braves in 1992. When I met Sid after the event, he told me he had someone he'd like for me to talk with.

"We have this kid, Joel Goddard, who does the music for our [the Braves'] weekly Bible study. We're trying to help him, and I'd like for you to talk to him. I'm going to tell Jon Cunningham to call you this afternoon," he said.

I did get a call from Jon Cunningham, who was a wealthy businessman with a truly miraculous testimony of being healed of cancer. Jon, I would later learn, had literally been at death's door with testicular cancer, the next one expected to die on the floor of the alternative medicine hospital in Mexico, which he had gone to as his last hope. In that desperate hour, Jon had told God that if he would spare his life, everything Jon had was God's, and he would use it to whatever ends would be pleasing to the Lord. Instead of dying as the doctors were certain he would, Jon began to regain strength day by day, and inexplicably to the doctors, his tumors began to shrink and go away.

Jon, just a shell of a man in the Mexican hospital, was ultimately totally and completely restored to health by God's hand. Jon kept true to his word and sought to help people in whatever ways and by whatever means he could. He had taken the young Joel Goddard under his wing and was helping Joel with his career. Several of the Braves players were behind Joel as well, desiring for him a larger platform for his music and ministry. I soon met with Joel and Jon, and plans were made for me to produce an album for Joel. I sensed his sincerity and humbleness of heart and could understand why he had so many ardent supporters. He had written some good original material and was eager to record it. I was just finishing up a project for Darrell Ritchie, another Christian artist whom I would produce through a couple of decades. After Darrell's project was finished, we set about working on Joel's. He and Jon would come to the studio each day, Jon with a briefcase of work to be done and several cell phones, which he managed skillfully.

As we were working on the project, various Atlanta Braves players would randomly show up at the studio on their off days to watch and hear what was being done. Jon Smoltz, Tim Cash, and Terry Pendleton were a few of them, names well known to anyone who was an Atlanta Braves fan at that time. As we were wrapping up Joel's project, plans were made to work a development deal with Cyndi Thomson and to cut some tracks with her in Nashville. It was a natural progression in our relationship with Cyndi. My partners saw the potential in her and were eager to get on board and benefit from Cyndi's abilities, which we all thought would propel her to stardom in the country market.

When I got back from the Nashville session with Cyndi, my partners had a surprise for me. They wanted me to sign an agreement stating that if they chose to pull out of the business, they would be entitled to all the equipment, leaving me with nothing. I appreciated the money they had put into the business, but much of the equipment was mine before they ever came into the business, and the business brought in was in large part due to my musical, production, and engineering capabilities, and my reputation before they ever entered into partnership with me. The two were not musicians and made no creative contribution to the business in that way. I had for some time begun to feel that I had become an employee of theirs instead of a partner and the one who had started and built the business in the first place. I had definite misgivings about signing all the equipment over to them, even though they were putting in money, which allowed us to do things we could not have done without it. I ultimately refused to sign the document, and they walked away, saying they would cut their losses, and they ended our partnership in a single afternoon. I suppose they were already wanting to get out and were going to try and sell my equipment to get back some of the money they had put in. When that didn't work, they just decided to walk away. Michelle and I were totally shocked, to say the least. We had no idea how things were going to work without them but had faith that the business would continue to grow as it had in the past. The year did pass, and thankfully the work kept coming.

One day in October, I came in to work and had not been there long when I heard a commotion out front. I opened the door, and the fire marshal, whom I knew, was standing just in front of it. A crew was in the process of putting flags and cones up around the building.

"What's going on?" I asked.

"We're here to condemn the building," he said without preamble.

"What are you talking about?" I demanded in disbelief, once again experiencing the sinking feeling that I had when the Home Federal building had flooded.

"A storm drain has collapsed under the street and is eroding the foundation of the building. It's not safe," he said with certainty in his voice.

I was incredulous, disbelieving that any such thing was happening underneath our feet. We had sensed no sinking of foundation, movement, or trouble of any kind. It was hard not to feel defeated as they put up the signs on each door stating that the building was condemned and unsafe for occupancy. I could no longer have people come in the studio and was not even supposed to be in there myself. All work came to a screeching halt, and all income with it.

Somehow, by the grace of God and generosity of our friends and family, bills were paid, and we still had groceries during this time of transition. There were many acts of kindness and support, not the least of which was a generous gift from some of the people at First Baptist Church Merritt Island, Florida. I had worked with people from this church on a musical called *The Watchman Call* around the time of the Debbie Nagal project. Debbie had ties to FBC Merritt Island, and that is how I became connected with Angie Kolsch, the writer of the musical. They heard of our misfortune and took up money for a gift that would help see us through those months of relocation.

As with many things that at first seem hopeless, the building condemnation turned out to be a blessing in disguise. We received a small settlement from the insurance company of the city of Gainesville, which helped us relocate and build out another location, which was even better, nicer, and newer than what we had before. We had to cancel sessions abruptly when we were shut down, so we had people waiting in line before we even reopened. One of those projects was a "live" album for Joel Goddard. Everyone involved had been quite pleased with his first project, so I was again to work with Joel, Jon, and whatever Atlanta Braves players decided to show up throughout the process. For this project, we brought some A-list players down from Nashville to record the live album at Hebron

Baptist Church. My old friend Tom Hemby came down, as well as Craig Nelson, Steve Brewster, and Byron Hagan. I played keyboards as well. It was a great night of worship; there was a lot of excitement about Joel and his future.

Immediately on the heels of Joel's project, I started on yet another album for Rick Pruett. The group had added a new member, David Ragsdale, whom I knew from my days on the road with the Fort Mountain Boys. David had most recently been a member of the band Kansas but had played fiddle for Leon Everett in the past and had been on the cruise with us. He was an excellent player and musician. He was a delight to work with, although other members of Rick's group were quite the opposite. One of the members who was to co-produce the album was especially difficult to work with. It was his involvement that had delayed the previous project being completed and would make this project equally as challenging. Soon it was a toxic environment, and it was clearly not producing the result that any of us wanted. We parted ways, and that particular album was never completed.

Around this time, another Christian artist/songwriter with ties to Merritt Island, Florida, came to my attention. Karen Klein was an extremely talented young lady whom I would describe as a very "vibey" individual. She had a unique vocal ability, and her songwriting was strong as well, especially when paired with other strong writers. Here, Jon Cunningham came back into the picture. He had heard of Karen and wanted to fund a project for her and aid in her development as an artist. Plans were made to begin her project. We again brought some A-list players and vocalists down from Nashville to work on the project, and it was a very creative, innovative project. I thought it was going to be a huge success. We did have the interest of some record labels at that time, but as sometimes happens, it never materialized into an offer of a contract for Karen.

No story of my life would be complete without mentioning Chris Orr. Michelle and I had watched Chris grow up at Blackshear Place and had heard him developing his vocal ability over the years, although we did not know him that well. He walked in the studio one day and said he wanted to record an album. He was very talented, but I was not sure he was ready for that yet, and not sure he would understand what kind of money it would take to do what he was asking. With these thoughts going through my head, I spent a little while trying to discourage him from pursuing his plans. Through our discussion, I learned his grandparents were prepared to pay for the album to be done. The very next day, Chris brought a deposit for the studio time. I began to set about finding some good original songs for him with the idea that we would do some old classics as well.

Michelle was still in school at Brenau, and in the class behind her was a delightful, sweet girl, a preacher's daughter named Marla Boykin, who Michelle felt would be a perfect match for Chris. Ironically, Marla, who was from South Georgia, had started going to church at Blackshear Place, and she and Chris had already noticed each other even before we attempted to set them up. They began their friendship, which would blossom, and they would eventually marry. Shortly after Chris had completed his first album, he decided he needed to do an album that was more praise-and-worship-driven in musical style. He was trying to get bookings in churches and for various events and was doing more of that style of music when he did live engagements. We had a larger budget this time and brought in some local musicians, Paul Smith on bass and Ashley Appling on drums, to give it the feel we were looking for. I played the other instruments, and we all seemed to click together. We ended up going out with Chris on live dates and were more or less his band for a couple of years. Chris would have his periods of discouragement, when bookings were slow, and would come in the studio announcing that he thought he needed to quit and get a job at UPS. I'd try to bolster his confidence, telling him to hold on; I thought he was about to be really busy.

"Let's go get something to eat. It'll make you feel better," I would often say when he expressed these feelings.

Somehow the Prairie Peppers from Longhorn Steakhouse seemed to hearten him through the dark times, and he did hang on until the days he became really busy. Those days did come, and Chris was in demand for events all over the country. One of the events we did was the Ohio statewide Youth Evangelism Conference.

On the day after Christmas of 2000, we were on a 6:00 a.m. flight to Washington, where we would then connect to a flight to Akron, Ohio, to play at the event. It was twelve degrees when we got there, with heavy snow. The snow and frigid temperatures continued the entire week. It was cold for a bunch of Georgia boys, but we didn't let the frigid conditions keep us from getting into some mischief. We had rented a Ford Focus at the airport, and after that week, I understood why my dad always said never to buy a car that had been in a rental fleet. We more or less used that little car as a snowmobile, even taking it off road.

The camp where we were was in a rural area around Seneca Lake, with lots of farmland. Our responsibilities at the camp, while integral, were limited to playing at the morning and evening sessions, so we had a lot of free time on our hands. One day coming back from town, our drummer, Ashley, was driving. He was always the most daring and adventuresome of the group. He pulled into a large empty parking lot with the idea of doing doughnuts on the snow and ice. He floored it and pulled up hard on the emergency brake. We spun around with the force of a ride at Six Flags, and then it was on. Each of the band members had their turn; it was sort of like *The Dukes of Hazzard on Ice*. I was the eldest of the group, and even though I was joining in the fun, I didn't think it was wise for me to get behind the wheel. After all, I was a husband and father of one, with another one on the way. We had found out in November that we were expecting another baby due in early July.

"Mark, it's your turn," somebody piped up.

I guess they honestly didn't see how it could be any more dangerous with me at the wheel than anybody else under the current conditions. After a moment's hesitation, I got in the driver's seat, buckled up, and put the gas to the floor. I pulled up on the brake, and we did a beautiful doughnut. Right when I finished, none other than the camp director pulled up in his SUV. He was a good sport himself, a fun-loving sort of a guy, and had a good rapport with us from the start.

"Aww, man, I ain't believin' this. That's classic. Got the blind guy doin' doughnuts," he quipped.

We literally ran the wheels off the poor car, one of the tires pulling away from the wheel before the week was over. We also—I'm ashamed to say—threw some fireworks from the windows of the car in a deserted area. It doesn't do for a bunch of guys to go out on the road without women to keep them straight. They digress into the little boys still deep within.

The studio continued to be busy, and varied opportunities came throughout the year. I had the chance to work on Congressman Nathan Deal's commercials for his campaign. I had worked on his previous campaign for Congress when he was still a state senator from Georgia. He would ultimately become a twice-elected governor of our state. I worked in conjunction with Sawyer, Riley, Compton, a large ad agency in Atlanta with Gainesville ties. While working on Nathan's campaign, I asked Richard Riley, one of the partners in the ad agency, about an old friend Greg Smith. He told me Greg had left the firm and that I should contact him. I soon reconnected with Greg. He had actually been let go after twenty-one years at Sawyer, Riley, Compton because of downsizing. He had been given an adequate severance package, which was a help to him during the time he was exploring new opportunities. We discussed the idea of Greg coming to work with me. I was the musical creative but knew I would benefit from the talents and creativity of someone with a background in advertising and who was also a strong musician. Over the course of the next several weeks, Greg came to observe the goings-on and work at the studio and determined he'd like to be in partnership in the business. I was eager to have a partner who could bring expertise in areas other than just money matters, and I welcomed the new opportunity. A new chapter for Crosstown Sound began.

One of the first projects we worked on after Greg joined us was for an artist named Kecia Garland. I had worked with Kecia off and on since she was a girl in college and was in the Miss Georgia pageant. She had married and was entering a new phase of life. Kecia had been working with renowned vocal coach Jan Smith, who was well known at the time but would rise to real prominence in later years after working with artists such as Usher, Justin Bieber, Jennifer Nettles, and so many others. Jan came up to the studio to produce

Kecia's vocals. The album was a crossover country/Christian album, and Kecia experienced a great deal of success with it.

It was in 2000 that we learned Cyndi Thomson had signed with Capitol Records. They had apparently signed her after hearing her sing just three songs. I guess they heard what I had heard all those years ago when she was just fifteen and came to record for the very first time. Cyndi had hooked up with songwriter Tommy Lee James, and in 2000, James introduced her to Capitol Records, Nashville. Cyndi had never written before, but James had agreed to work with her on her songwriting. She ended up cowriting eight of the eleven songs on her debut album *My World*, which would release on July 31, 2001. It made quite a splash and became the best-selling debut album by a female country singer since LeAnn Rimes's album *Blue* was released in 1996. The album went gold after ten months. Her leadoff single, "What I Really Meant to Say," broke all kinds of records. It looked like her dreams had finally come true. I'll have to say I was not at all surprised.

Other opportunities came that year, such as working with Fernando Aragon again and playing some live shows with him. We had the chance to play a show for Shaw Industries at Disney World, where Warren Buffet was in attendance. In early June, I went to Boston to produce a show for a Fortune 500 company, Heidrick & Struggles.

Chapter 21

Oh, Baby!

I was concerned that I had to travel to Boston because this was getting close to Michelle's due date, and given her preterm birth with Graham, there were fears that this baby would come early as well. We had learned, to our complete joy, that the baby was a girl. As we got closer to the due date, that little girl remained in the position she was in, what they call "frank breech," where she was in the opposite position she should have been in to be born. She was folded up with her head and feet beside each other, and her bottom was where her head should have been. If she remained in this position, a C-section was to be scheduled because babies can rarely be turned when they are in this particular position.

In May, Michelle had reached a long-worked-for milestone and graduated from the occupational therapy program at Brenau University, summa cum laude, the highest honor. No small feat, especially with a family to care for while she was completing her studies. She always jokingly said she was going to cartwheel across the stage when she finally finished, but at eight months pregnant, her condition prevented it! It was a very proud moment for all of us seeing her graduate. Michelle's mother and dad, Ray and Sarah, had supported us a great deal during this time, providing childcare for Graham and paying for Michelle's tuition to return to school. They could not have been prouder.

As the weeks drew closer to Michelle's due date, the baby, whom we had decided to name Macy, remained in the position she had evidently become comfortable in, and a C-section was scheduled for

June 29. Macy's name was actually suggested by Graham, then five years old.

"I know what we can name our baby. Let's name her Macy!" he piped up.

"Oh, I like that name! Do you know a 'Macy'?" Michelle asked, thinking there might be a girl named Macy in his class at school we had not heard about.

"No. You know the department store? And she'd always have her own parade!" he said, evidently thinking of the Macy's Thanksgiving Day Parade.

We both laughed at that and thought it would be a neat story for her to have regarding her name, so Macy it was.

On the evening of June 28, we went to eat at Macaroni Grill, Michelle's favorite restaurant, for the last time as a family of three. We were nervous but excited about what the next day would bring. The C-section was scheduled for the twenty-ninth, but we were to be "on call" as far as the time we would need to be there. We rose early with anticipation, but the morning seemed to drag by, and the call did not come until about 11:30 a.m. We arrived at the hospital, and Michelle was prepped and ready to go into the operating room about 12:45 a.m. I had to get into scrubs as well. Michelle was a bit apprehensive as the epidural was administered, and I was trying to remain outwardly calm for her sake. Dr. Connor soon put us at ease, however, as the procedure began, having delivered thousands of babies in his career. The whole procedure did not take long, and at 1:18 p.m., Macy Lynn Dowdy was delivered. Even though it was a surgical procedure, there was still that quietness, that silent moment, when I felt the wind of the Spirit, like it was delivering her soul into the room.

The silence lasted only a moment, though, until Macy burst forth with a lusty cry, bearing witness to a set of lungs and vocal cords that would become her trademark!

Dr. Connor held her up proudly for us to see. This was our dark-haired girl, beautiful in every way. She weighed a healthy seven pounds. The nurses whisked Macy away to get her cleaned up and checked out. I followed, talking to her the entire time they were working with her.

"Wow, Macy, you're finally here!" I told her with a full heart.

Soon I went back to Michelle in recovery, and she was doing well also. She was moved to a room, and we waited on them to bring Macy up to us. The nurse finally brought her in. The room full of people all agreed that she was the most beautiful baby they had ever seen, with her dark hair and unusually long eyelashes. She was passed around as everyone enjoyed holding her, especially Graham, who could not seem to get enough of his new little sister. Michelle spent three days in the hospital, and we brought Macy home on July 2. It was a very different experience from what we had gone through with Graham.

Macy was a good baby, and she slept well too. When she was awake, we would spend time "playing" with her, enjoying every minute of it. When she was asleep, we would both watch her. I would often kneel by the basinet to see her better, saying a prayer for her while I was on my knees. Macy's "fussy" time of day was from about 5–7:00 p.m., when she would cry more than other times. I would often come in from work when she was crying, and I'd take her in my arms and walk around and sing to her. It always seemed to calm her down. It didn't take long for us to settle into a routine with a fourth member of the family—she made everything feel complete.

Life had a comfortableness about it, and we were enjoying the thought of the upcoming Thanksgiving and Christmas season with Macy and the new joy she had brought to our family. It was a cool North Georgia morning on September 11, and it started like any other. But it would turn into a day no one who lived through it would ever forget. I had the TV on while I was shaving and getting ready for work. I remember so many things about that day—and the news of the first plane hitting the World Trade Center being delivered. I was watching Fox News and remember that, at first, they thought it was a small plane that had crashed into the building, but then determined it was, in fact, a commercial jetliner. It wasn't long before the speculation of terrorism began to be discussed, and then the other terrible events unfolded. It was like something out of a movie, and with each passing minute, our hearts sank deeper with the knowledge that things would never be quite the same again. Our concern for the people affected was paramount, and the heaviness of heart which ensued is hard to describe. Michelle had already taken Graham to school at that point, and we were concerned about his safety. It was a time when you just wanted all your loved ones around you, not knowing what was going to happen next.

I went into work a little late, but we didn't get anything done that day. Everyone was glued to the TV. In churches, people were meeting to pray. A prayer service was scheduled at Blackshear Place that evening, and I played for it. It was a time that caused reflection. For many, it drove them back to or deeper into their faith, while for others, it led to questions about how God could allow something like this to happen. I would not begin to have the answer to that question but did have a sense of the resolve that the country would get through it. I didn't know how or when, but I knew that we would.

Despite the gloom that had settled over us, we went on with work as scheduled. Chris Orr was slated to record a live album on September 22, and rehearsals for that week had already been planned. We recorded it at Pearce Auditorium at Brenau University on the scheduled date, although life was far from returning to any kind of normalcy. It was a busy time from then until the end of the year with various projects. We got through the holidays, which were subdued that year.

Chapter 22

OBEDIENCE

The year 2002 was one of the busiest on record, with one project after another filling up the year. With our growing family and growing business, the year seemed to pass by with lightning speed. At the end of the year, I was getting ready to go down to Florida to play for another Shaw Industries show. Michelle dropped me off at the studio the first Monday morning back after the holidays, and I was the first one there. I had a small office in the back, and I would often sit at my desk and have my quiet time with God in the morning before the others arrived. This particular morning, I felt that familiar tugging at my heart. I didn't even know what it meant, but I felt I needed to pray what I would describe as a prayer of obedience.

"Lord, I really don't even know what this means, but I feel like I need to tell you and say out loud that whatever you want me to do, I'll do."

Little did I know how that prayer would change my life and my family's life for years to come. We had the hope of a promising year, with the prospects of some good projects. There were several projects on the line for the start of the year, and one group had already paid a deposit of $5,000. To our surprise, they called and informed us they were not going to be able to record the project and asked for their deposit money back. That is exactly why we asked for deposits, so people would take booking the studio time seriously and would be much less likely to try and back out at the last minute, leaving us hanging. We made it clear, in writing, that the deposit was nonrefundable. However, due to the circumstances around their cancellation, we felt compelled to honor their request and refund the deposit. So this meant we were out the deposit, plus the rest of the money for the project. Oddly enough, the other projects, which were almost sure things, began to fall through one by one. It was very unusual, and I just didn't know what to make of it. All of this happened after my prayer, but I didn't really make the connection at the time as we so often don't when things are happening in real time.

Around this same time, I had begun to think about my vision and what new options might be available to me. I was thirty-seven; it had been twenty-seven years since my last surgery. I went to see Dr. Bill Morrison, an ophthalmologist whose daughter I had worked with on a project recently. He sent me to another eye surgeon in town, who subsequently sent me to Emory University Hospital to see Dr. George Waring. Since Emory is a teaching hospital, within five minutes of me being in the exam room, a team of doctors came in. I think the more unusual the case, the bigger the crowd it attracts. They all seemed to be discussing my case.

"Do you think he is?" I heard one of them say.

"What am I?" I asked, curious at such a question.

They were discussing whether I would be a candidate for a stem cell implant, which would precede a new cornea transplant. Dr. Diane Song was in the room, and it was she who explained to me that during development, the stem cells that give rise to the cornea were not there for it to form properly in my case. So maybe this was the missing piece and why all the other transplants had failed. We spent some time in discussion about what the surgeries would entail. First, the stem cell transplant would be done. They would remove the old opaque cornea, scrape the epithelial cells off, and put the stem cell tissue in place. This would have to "take" and not show signs of rejection; otherwise, there would be no point in doing the cornea transplant. Dr. Song also told me that she would want me on some pretty heavy antirejection drugs, given my history of rejecting so many corneas.

It was a lot to take in; I told them I needed some time to think about all the information they had given me. I decided to take a month to pray and do some research about both procedures. I had many questions, like the success rate, the outcomes, and what others who had had this done experienced.

During that month, we did pray, and we gathered as much information as we could about these particular surgeries. We learned that the "souped up" cornea transplant had actually been done for about ten years, typically with great success. There were varying outcomes as far as visual acuity, but most outcomes were to the positive at least to some degree. There is always a risk, however, with any procedure; and given my history, I didn't take it lightly. I knew I had the one eye to play with, and I had to weigh the possibility that what little vision I did have might be taken away due to failure of the procedure or through some sort of unforeseen complication.

Finally, though, at the end of the month, the pros seemed to outweigh the cons, and I really felt a peace about going ahead with the procedures. I called Emory in early March and told them I wanted to schedule the first transplant. The date was set for April 9, 2003. We began to let our friends and family know about the surgery and ask for their prayers.

The very same week, I received phone calls from three different churches that needed an interim worship leader, and each asked if I would consider filling the position. To the first two, I automatically said no. At the time, I was playing at Blackshear Place weekly and did not connect those calls to my earlier prayer of obedience just yet. I didn't even entertain the thought of saying yes, thinking that it would take too much time away from the studio. A leader from the third church called that week, and after telling me they had a need for an interim worship leader, she made what to me was an unusual statement.

"Before you say no, just come and talk with us," said Deborah Lowe.

Why would she start off the conversation like that? I thought.

It was like she knew I was going to say no. By this time, the light was dawning on me, and I thought maybe the Lord was nudging me out of my comfort zone, putting the sincerity of my prayer to the test. I agreed to meet with the people from Dunwoody but could not conceive of a way it could work, with my responsibilities at the studio. Michelle and I drove down to Dunwoody (about a forty-five-minute drive with no traffic) on a Monday evening. We spent some time around the piano, singing and talking with the leadership team responsible for filling the position. We came away with a good feeling about it, but we needed some time to think through how we could make it work, and they needed some time to think about how much time they would require of me.

I was preparing for the stem cell surgery and had been on the antirejection meds for about two weeks. Some of these medications made me very edgy, and I was on a high dose of all of them. I took prednisone, which was the worst offender, and I felt must be of the devil. I was also on CellCept, which lowers one's immunity, and an oral cyclosporin. It was a real struggle to maintain my cool when these medications made me feel like I wanted to lash out at everyone. I was told that the stem cell surgery would not be a difficult one and that I would be able to go back to work in a couple of days. I was totally unprepared for how the meds and this particular surgery would affect me.

The stem cell implant took place on April 9 as scheduled, without much fanfare. It was an outpatient procedure, and I went in feeling upbeat. Michelle and I stayed in a conference center near the campus that night so we would be close by in the morning for my post-op appointment. The first day and night, I was nauseated, but not in a lot of pain since my eye was still numb from the surgery. Dr. Song examined me the next day and said everything looked good. We came home expecting an uneventful recovery period of a couple of days.

The next few days, however, turned out to be torturous as the pain started to kick in, and combined with the effects of the antirejection meds, it sent me into a downward spiral. I kept thinking something had to be wrong because I was in so much pain. I couldn't even open my eye, which meant I was totally blind at that point. I had not been able to sleep well since the first night following the surgery when I was so drugged up. We went back to Emory for them to check me again when the pain was still with me after several days. Dr. Song was on a two-week trip, but the doctor on call assured me everything was fine, and any problem I was experiencing was all in my head.

Two days later, I came unglued. I was still terribly depressed, unable to see at all, but I tried to go back to work. My head felt like it was going to explode most of the time. One day it felt so tight from pressure I thought something was about to happen to me. The tighter it felt, the more agitated I got. I went into Greg's office almost in a panic.

"You've got to take me to the hospital," I said anxiously.

He took me to Lanier Park Hospital, where Michelle was working at the time, and she met us at the ER. The emergency-room doctor took a look, although by his own admission, this kind of eye situation was out of his league. He did, however, do a good job of talking me down from my panicked state.

"I don't know a lot about the procedure you've had, but you've just got to hang on. It's all going to be worth it in the end," he said with compassion. He spent some time talking to me, reassuring me with his calm manner and belief that all was well.

He prescribed for me a sleeping pill, and that night I had the best night's sleep I'd had in over a week. The next morning, I started pulling out of it, but still had to fight my way back, willing myself to keep going. Things got better day by day, and by Easter Sunday, I was feeling like I could return to the world, even playing at Blackshear Place that morning. We went back to Emory on the twenty-second and saw Dr. Song. She had heard what a rough time I'd had while she'd been gone, and she was rather surprised.

By that time, I was feeling better both physically and mentally, but was still not convinced that everything was okay with the transplant. She sat down in front of me and examined my eye. She leaned back in her chair.

"I don't believe this!" she said.

Do you mean that in a good way or a bad way? I thought.

"It usually takes four to six weeks for healing, but the first layer of your epithelium is already healed after just two weeks!" she said with pleasure.

I got chills when she said that, knowing I had been the recipient of a miracle, even though I'd been through the fire to get it. It appeared my body was not rejecting the cells but had actually gone into overdrive in accepting them.

The people from Dunwoody Baptist had called during those awful days, which I would later refer to as "hell week," to see if I would come to lead worship on a Sunday sometime soon. Somehow I was able to talk to them and even agreed to go down and lead on April 27. I was still not totally back to normal on the twenty-seventh, but I felt well enough to keep my commitment. It was a great Sunday, and I was glad to be able to return to some semblance of normalcy. They called a couple of weeks later and offered me the interim position, which was to last six months. They wanted me in the office three days per week, in addition to Sundays.

There were a couple of obstacles for me in taking the position. First and foremost was the studio and not wanting to let my partners down. By this time, we had another partner, Linda Rowe, whom I had worked with in the past. I couldn't exactly be in two places at once and didn't see how I could fulfill my obligations at the studio and do the worship position too. Secondly, I would need transportation to Dunwoody, which was off I-285, about fifty miles from home. I-285 is notorious for being backed up during rush hour, easily turning an hour-long trip into about two and a half hours. Michelle was working part-time at the hospital, and we had Graham and Macy at that point. It would not have been practical for Michelle to drive me during the week.

I felt strongly impressed that I should take this opportunity, however, and that it was directly related to the prayer I had prayed just a few months earlier. I discussed this with my partners, who were like-minded believers. The funny thing was that business had come to a screeching halt. After the busiest two years I'd ever had, the projects seemed to have dried up. My partners both agreed that I should take the position, even likening me to Jonah and expressing their belief that this might be the reason business was so slow. I think they wanted to "throw Jonah from the boat" to see if things would turn around. I had their blessing to accept the position since it would allow me to be in the studio two days a week and on Saturdays if necessary.

I still had the problem of transportation, however. In talking with the folks at Dunwoody, they informed me that they also needed to get an assistant for me and asked if I knew anyone that might be interested. This sparked an idea that I would have not thought possible. At the time, we had Ryan Roebuck working with us as an engineer. Ryan had interned at the studio to fulfill the requirements of the commercial music program at Georgia State University, from which he graduated. He stayed on with us after he completed his degree since we had plenty for him to do. With business being so slow during that time, however, his future with us was not looking as bright. Ryan was about ten years younger than me, and I had watched him grow up at Blackshear Place Baptist through his teen years, so we had a long history. I discussed this opportunity with him and what it would involve. It was not merely a clerical position but would require working with technology, as well as with the music. It seemed to be a perfect fit, and since we had no projects on the books at the studio, it would provide a steady stream of income for the newly married Ryan. The team at Dunwoody was excited about Ryan coming on board as well, especially when they found out about his background.

With both the obstacles removed, I accepted the position, certain that God had paved the way for me and had made the "crooked places straight." I was excited for this new opportunity and the changes it brought with it. Ryan and I headed down to Dunwoody on May 14 for our first day on the job. I walked into my office, and before I even set down my briefcase or turned on the light, my mind went back to what Nanny had told me so many times all those years ago.

"You're going to be a preacher," she used to say.

"Well, Nanny, I guess you were right after all," I said, looking up.

Even though I wasn't "the preacher" delivering a spoken message, I was going to use my music in a new way to reach people with the hope that I had always known in my own life, the hope that had always sustained me. We immediately settled in and enjoyed life at

Dunwoody. I was in my element, using my production skills when I worked with the band and small praise choir. Our band was made up of paid members, so they were high-caliber players, but not members of Dunwoody. The church was in a time of transition and also had an interim pastor. His name was Alan Jackson, and he was a professor at New Orleans Baptist Theological Seminary. The church would fly him in each week to deliver the message in the Sunday service, but he was not involved in the day-to-day activities or inner workings of the church.

We formed some deep friendships while there, and it would be these people who would walk with us most closely through the next surgery. I was still on all the antirejection meds during this time but was learning to deal with how they made me feel. With each passing week, I felt better about the stem cells not rejecting. The original plan was to wait about six months for the cornea transplant following the stem cell implant, but the surgery was scheduled for September 17, 2003, a bit sooner than we expected.

Chapter 23

CALLING FOR YOU AND FOR ME

The Sunday before the surgery, the people at Dunwoody Baptist had a special time of prayer for me. One of the leadership team, a young man named Matt Garland, read the scripture depicting blind Bartimaeus from Mark chapter 10.

> They called out to the blind man and said, "Don't be afraid! Come on! He is calling for you." The man threw off his coat as he jumped up and ran to Jesus. Jesus asked, "What do you want me to do for you?" The blind man answered, "Master, I want to see!" Jesus told him, "You may go. Your eyes are healed because of your faith." Right away the man could see, and he went down the road with Jesus.

Matt read the story with great emotion and then prayed earnestly over me. "Lord, what do we want? What does Mark want? We want him to see! He wants to be able to see, just like blind Bartimaeus. So we ask you to be with Mark and with the surgeon's hands and bring about the healing we so desperately want. And we'll be careful to give you all the glory for it."

Hearts, minds, and voices all joined in prayer asking for my healing. It was a beautiful, emotional time, and I won't ever forget it.

I also learned that some of the members of First Baptist Church of Gainesville had a prayer service at the church for me. Even though

I wasn't there, I could just imagine the prayers of those dear saints going up on my behalf. I had been put on various prayer lists around the country as well. This was before the days of social media and everything being known via the internet, so it was a little more remarkable that my story got shared so far and wide.

It was with this sort of anticipation that we went into the surgery. I was hopeful but not unaware of the risk I was taking. Michelle and I had discussed the fact that if the surgery was successful and I received my healing, God would receive all the glory. But what if the surgery failed, we asked ourselves? Would God still be on his throne? We knew we had to be willing to either praise him for the miracle or thank him for the thorn, whichever came.

Chapter 24

Waiting

The surgery was over in a couple of hours, and Dr. Song came to report to my family.

"Wow, I don't recall ever seeing such a big group here for an eye surgery," she told Michelle as she looked around the waiting room. "The surgery went really well, so we'll just have to wait and see until in the morning when the patch comes off."

Michelle recalls her being amused at my chatter during the procedure when she shared a glimpse of what had gone on in the operating room.

"He is so funny. He was just talking throughout the surgery, and we all thought he should be more out of it, but we asked him his social security number, and he just rattled it right off!" she said.

I spent a brief time in the recovery area where they gave me some crackers and ginger ale. I was deemed ready to go and realized all of a sudden how hungry I was. Michelle and I were to spend the night in one of the rooms of the Emory Conference Center so we wouldn't have to make the fifty-mile trip from Atlanta to Gainesville and then back the next morning. Also, if something were to happen in the night, a hemorrhage or anything like that, I would be right there at the hospital. We were planning to have room service when we got to the hotel, but I was feeling upbeat and asked Michelle and my parents if they wanted to go and eat in the restaurant at the hotel. They were surprised, thinking I would not be feeling up to that, in addition to the fact that my eye was patched and I couldn't see at all. But I was pumped up and feeling like I wanted to do something besides just sit in the hotel room. We had a pleasant meal and then headed back to the hotel for what we hoped would be an uneventful night.

I remember the Braves game being on television that evening, and I always loved the Atlanta Braves and watching baseball. I was lying there in bed, just listening to the game.

What is it going to be like in the morning? I thought.

Even at that point, under the patch, I kept seeing light, what seemed like a significant amount of light; and to me, that was a very hopeful sign. I remember all the questions running through my mind.

What will things really look like? How will this change my life? Will I be able to drive? Will this make me a better musician or worse? How will it change my musicality?

Most of all, I was thinking about my family and seeing them, wondering if Michelle's hair was really the golden color I thought it was. I wondered about my children, and I remember thinking about Macy in particular, then two years old. People always talked about her big beautiful eyes and her unusually long lashes. I wanted to see those eyes for myself, right down to the long lashes.

People would always ask me, "What can you see?"

I guess I would describe it as looking through a windshield with ice on it or a steamed-up shower door. I could see light and forms of things, but I couldn't see distinctly. I could see color fairly well as long as it was up close. I did pick out my own clothes; people always seem to wonder about that—I could definitely match my socks to my shirt! When the Scripture talks of the blind man saying, "I see men like trees walking," that is a fairly apt description of what my world was like. So I was waiting on my healing, just like that man. Maybe, just maybe, this was my time.

Chapter 25

Let There Be Light

The night passed well with no problems. We got ready with eager anticipation of what the next few hours would hold. The Emory Eye Center was about five minutes away. We utilized the valet parking so we could just go right in, and I wouldn't have to walk a long way. We went to the third floor, and before long, we were back in an examination room. The technician came in to take the bandage off. I guess that was a technician's job, but I thought it was terribly anticlimactic that Dr. Song did not come in to remove the bandage herself. After all, this could be a life-changing event! The tech's fingers gingerly worked off the tape and the bandage with it.

"All right, open your eye and tell me what you see," she said calmly.

I opened my eye with difficulty and was immediately bombarded with what appeared like tiny stars and dots.

"Oh my God, something went wrong!" I thought desperately.

As a matter of fact, I didn't just think it—I said it out loud!

"Okay. What do you see?" said the tech, retaining her calm demeanor despite my excitement.

"I just see all kinds of stars and dots, and it doesn't make sense," I said, feeling the desperation and disappointment stealing over me.

The only light on in the room was a small light over the exam chair. The overhead light wasn't even on yet. I knew there was very little light on in the room, but it seemed so bright in there to me.

"Just take a minute and focus on something, something that you know," she said firmly.

I held up two fingers, like a peace sign in front of my eye, and it was then that I saw what I was looking for. I could see my individual fingers. I kept moving them farther and farther back, as far as my arm could reach, and I could still see the individual fingers. The stars and dots began to be replaced by clearer images as I focused in on various objects.

Wow, this is fantastic! I thought. I began to get really excited then.

I looked and saw Michelle sitting across the room, about four or five feet away.

"Can you see me? Can you see my face?" she asked.

"I can see you *have* a face," I said, not trying to be funny but still trying to take it all in.

Probably not the reaction she was looking for, but I could not see her face in detail at that point.

I was overwhelmed. Dr. Song came in and turned the lights on. I was still adjusting to the onslaught of all the visual input, and it was confusing yet wonderful. I could see Dr. Song's long black hair against her white lab coat. I could also see her prescription pad on the desk. I could see the light switch across the room. Little things were coming into focus. She asked what I could see, and I enumerated all those things. She was excited but not overly so, but it was okay because I was excited enough for the both of us. She examined me and said that all was well, and the graft looked good. I was to come back for her to check me in a week.

It was a different experience walking out of that room and being able to see where I was going. It was a whole big wide world, and I was ready to see it and experience it in a whole new way. The drive home was amazing. I would pick out a car and see how long I could see it as it would pass by. Michelle said I sounded like Larry Munson, the great radio announcer for the Georgia Bulldogs as I said repeatedly, and with no small measure of excitement, "I see it! I still see it! I STILL SEE IT!"

I could see bridges and overpasses from a pretty far distance as well. Michelle and I decided to stop and eat lunch before going home. Every experience was new, and I was telling Michelle everything I saw.

"I see the salsa in the bowl," I said. "I see my straw." I looked across the table. "I see your straw too!" I said excitedly. All these little things that I could not imagine seeing before were now visible to me.

I wanted to have a few minutes at home to acclimate myself to my surroundings and take everything in before the children came home. I walked around the house and looked at each room. I remember standing in our bedroom and looking across the hall into Macy's room. I could see toys on the floor and pictures on the wall. I was still not seeing things distinctly, but I was able to see objects at a much farther distance. I had to remember also that I had no glasses or correction of any kind yet either.

Graham and Macy were soon brought home by Michelle's mother and dad. I remember sitting in my chair and Graham coming and standing beside it.

"Don't you have a handsome boy, Mark?" asked Sarah.

"I sure do," I said, my heart overflowing with gratitude.

Macy was just two years old and could not fully comprehend what was going on, but she walked over to my chair and put her face right up next to mine. I could see clearly the beautiful face and eyes everyone always talked about. I was afraid to cry, afraid of damaging the sutures or the cornea, but I could have wept like a baby.

I felt so good, like I wanted to jump right back into life. It was very different from the previous surgery, even with the pain level and how my eye felt. I was ready to do things and see things I had not seen before. It was just a miracle. I remember thinking, *All this time, and it had to be now because I wouldn't have been ready before now.*

As exciting as everything was, I knew we were in the early stages, and the possibility of rejection was still very real. I took heart in the fact that the stem cells had healed well and had not rejected. However, the cornea was from another donor, of course, and my body had rejected so many corneas before. Each day that passed, however, brought more hope that the cornea would not reject.

I found myself having to rest my eye quite frequently, not just from discomfort but from "sensory overload." I was getting so much more input to my brain than I was accustomed to, and I had to "turn it off" sometimes. The stars and dots I initially saw, we would later determine, was my brain firing and registering light and input as it had never done before, or at least in a very long time since the keratoprosthesis many years ago. In the days after the surgery, I was "learning" to see. Even things like getting used to the proper timing of a handshake when I saw someone's arm coming toward mine to shake my hand were things I had to learn.

Days went by, one week, then two, and things continued to progress. There were no signs of rejection, and each day I would notice something new or be able to see something with greater acuity. One of the most memorable moments following the surgery was when I returned to Dunwoody to lead worship for the first time. People had watched me since I had been there walk across the stage with assistance, with someone to hand me my guitar. The first Sunday back, I did something I had never done before. I climbed the steps alone, walked across the stage to my guitar, picked it up, and turned to the audience to lead them. They were on their feet, clapping with thunderous applause. We had received our miracle. I knew they weren't standing for me, even though they were happy for me. They were standing and clapping for what God had done, and I did give him all the glory. I knew it was his greatness on display, and I knew it was he who had allowed me to have this indescribable gift.

Epilogue

We were told that the average life of a corneal transplant is five to ten years. We just passed the sixteen-year mark, and the graft is still clear and healthy. About a year after the transplant, I did have a cataract that formed due to all the steroid eye drops I had to take to maintain the transplant. I had surgery to have the cataract removed, as well as another procedure to regulate pressure in my eye.

As far as my vision, it has continued to improve through the years. I mentioned the process of "learning" how to see; that process continues even now. My increased vision has enabled me to do many things that were not possible before. One of the biggest positive changes is that I am able to walk around without assistance, even in unfamiliar places. At someplace like the airport, I would still need assistance for directions, but I would not have to hold on to anyone's arm.

Another huge gain is being able to use a computer for my music production. Gone are the days of the old reel-to-reel machines with which I was so comfortable. As things began to go digital, there was a great deal I could not do. Today I can read a computer screen with an enlarged font and work with ProTools and other music software with ease.

I guess the reader might wonder if I got to fulfill my dream of driving. Unfortunately, that was one dream that did not come true. A few years ago, Macy told me, "Dad, I think you could drive if it weren't for the other cars on the road!"

She's probably right, but I don't see them clearing the highways just for me anytime soon!

The reader may also wonder about the "prayer of obedience" and where it led us. I left Crosstown Sound in 2004 and, for the next seven years, served full-time on various church staffs from Lavonia, Georgia, to Alabama, and back to Gainesville, Georgia, to serve at the church where I was baptized as a ten-year-old boy. We met some amazing people along the way and would not trade those years for anything. We felt great purpose in what we were doing and were satisfied that we were where God wanted us at the time.

All the while, I kept my hand in production work. There always seemed to be people who would want me to produce something for them, and I was glad for the opportunities that came to do that. In 2010, I went back to studio and production work full-time, feeling that the Lord was leading me into a new season. Over the past several years, I have been privileged to work with many young artists, helping them edge a little closer to realizing their dreams. I also experienced a renewed passion for songwriting and wrote for Final Four Publishing in Nashville for a few years. I was able to further hone my craft with veteran songwriter Michael Puryear, who mentored me during that time.

While my work has had me weave in and out of producing various genres, I have always wanted the music I was involved in to count for something. The older I get, the more kingdom-minded I have become about making music that has an eternal purpose and perspective. It is with that passion and desire that Worship 360 was born. We formed Worship 360 as a collaboration of artists and speakers who go and share their gifts and provide nights of worship to raise awareness and funds for parachurch organizations seeking to be the hands and feet of Jesus in their communities. Worship 360 is in its infancy, but we are working with several amazing new artists and organizations and are excited about where we are headed. We pray that God will use us as we continually surrender our work, our days, our everything to him.

One song that has been central to my life and ministry is a song called "Moses," written by the great Ken Medema, also a blind composer and artist. Medema was prolific, particularly in the '60s and '70s, and anybody who has sung in a church choir is probably familiar with him. I was privileged to sit down with him at the piano and learn "Moses" when I was eighteen years old. I hesitate to refer to

"Moses" as just a "song" because it is so epic—so masterfully woven both lyrically and musically. It is a conversation between God and Moses, with Moses offering all the excuses why he can't do what God has called him to do, telling God all his weaknesses, and God ultimately showing Moses God's power through Moses's obedience to "throw down" the rod he was holding in his hand. The song then goes on to ask, "What do you hold in your hand? To whom or to what are you bound?" The last verse calls us to "throw it down"— anything that we are holding that we have not surrendered to God. I have had to, at various times in my life, "throw down" some hopes and dreams that may not have been what God wanted for me. I have thrown down my weaknesses as well, knowing that in my weakness, God is strong.

What about you, dear reader? What are you holding in your hand? What is holding you back from being fully surrendered to the life God wants you to have? If this book does nothing else, I pray it will give you encouragement to be bold in your faith, and with me, pray that prayer of obedience to follow his will, wherever it leads.

Klein; writer: David Bellamy; publisher: Bellamy Brothers, ASCAP; MCA/Curb 52446. Another platitude-filled paean to female pulchritude, in—and out—of bed.

——recommended——

KEITH STEGALL—Whatever Turns You On (2:42); producer: Kyle Lehning; writers: K. Stegall, D. Lowery; publishers: Blackwood/Stegall, BMI/Sheddhouse, ASCAP; Epic 34-04590. Stegall offers to play it any way—as long as it suits his lover.

TERRI GIBBS—Rocky Top (2:27); producer: Ed Penney; writers: Boudleaux Bryant, Felice Bryant; publisher: House of Bryant, BMI; MCA 52440. Good thing Gibbs has already left MCA; the world isn't waiting for the billionth version of this sing-along.

RAY STEVENS—I'm Kissin' You Goodbye (3:09); producer: Ray Stevens; writer: Ray Stevens; publisher: Ray Stevens, BMI; MCA 52451. It's a cross between bluegrass and novelty, but the explicit reference to French kissing is questionable.

PINKARD & BOWDEN—Mama, She's Lazy (3:24); producers: Pinkard & Bowden; writer: Kenny O'Dell; publisher: Kenny O'Dell, BMI; Warner Bros. 7-29205. A parody that should nicely balance the Judd's euphoria over their recent No. 1, "Mama He's Crazy."

MARK DOWDY—A Lady Afraid To Let Go (3:23); producer: Billy Strange; writers: Scott Phelps, Judy Mehaffey; publishers: Tapadero/Movieville, BMI; Soundwaves SW-4737-NSD. Soothing, concerned voice interpreting a modern dilemma. Label based in Nashville.

NARVEL FELTS—I'm Glad You Couldn't Sleep Last Night (3:08); producer: Johnny Morris; writers: Terry Skinner, J. L. Wallace, Steve Nathan; publishers: Hall-Clement/Jack & Bill, BMI/ASCAP; Evergreen EV-

DEAR MARK:

I'M SORRY IT HAS TAKEN ME SO LONG TO GET THESE TAPES TO YOU. JUDY AND ME HAVE BOTH BEEN DOWN WITH THE FLU SINCE YOU LEFT NASHVILLE. I UNDERSTAND FROM YOUR DAD THAT YOU HAVE HAD IT TOO. I'M SORRY TO HAVE ACTED AS YOUR CARRIER OF DISEASE. I HOPE YOU ARE FEELING BETTER NOW.

I HAVE ENCLOSED TWO CASSETTES WITH SIX SONGS ON EACH. YOU WILL FIND A WIDE VARIETY OF MATERIAL TO GO OVER. I DON'T WISH TO PRE-SUPPOSE WHAT YOU WILL LIKE OR DISLIKE IN THIS BATCH OF SONGS, SO I WON'T COMMENT ON ANY OF THEM EXCEPT TO SAY THAT THEY ARE ALL GOOD SONGS, WHICH COULD MAKE TERRIFIC RECORDS. ANY OF THE SONGS ON THESE TAPES COULD BE DONE VERY WELL BY YOU. I WAS VERY CAREFUL ABOUT LYRIC CONTENT, DUE TO YOUR AGE. I DON'T THINK ANY OF THE SONGS ARE TOO OLD IN THOUGHT FOR YOU TO PERFORM.

PLEASE LET ME KNOW IF YOU LIKE WHAT I HAVE SENT YOU, AND LET ME KNOW WHAT ABOUT THEM YOU PARTICULARLY LIKE AND WHY.

HOPING TO HEAR FROM YOU VERY SOON, I REMAIN

YOUR TRULY,

Billy

RETINA ASSOCIATES
ESTABLISHED 1951

C. L. SCHEPENS, M. D.
I. D. OKAMURA, M. D.
R. J. BROCKHURST, M. D.
J. W. McMEEL, M. D.

100 CHARLES RIVER PLAZA
CAMBRIDGE STREET
BOSTON, MASSACHUSETTS 02114
(617) 523-7810

H. M. FREEMAN, M. D.
R. O. PRUETT, M. D.
F. I. TOLENTINO, M. D.
T. HIROSE, M. D.

R. A. FIELD, M. D.
Endocrinologist

June 25, 1976

Mrs. Bobby E. Dowdy
P.O. Box 398
Gainesville, Georgia   30501

Dear Mrs. Dowdy:

Thank you for your letter of June 14. I appreciate having
some news concerning Mark. You can be very proud of him inasmuch as
I found him to be a child of exceptional courage and fortitude. With
those attributes I am sure that he will make his way in life no matter
how limited his vision may be. Please give him my very best regards
and once again let me commend you on being such wonderful parents to him.
In all the years that I have been in medicine, I have seen very few
parents that have gone to such length as you and Mr. Dowdy to save the
sight in their childs' eyes.

With my very best regards.

Sincerely yours,

H M Freeman

H. MacKenzie Freeman, M.D.

HMF/jac

About the Author

Mark Dowdy has more than thirty years of experience in the music industry as an engineer, producer, musician, and artist. Mark has a passion for worship, music, and for helping young artists find their voice. He has served churches in both Georgia and Alabama as worship pastor. Mark is the founder of Worship 360, an organization seeking to use music and evenings of worship to bring awareness to parachurch organizations seeking to be the hands and feet of Jesus in their communities. He and his wife, Michelle, live in Gainesville, Georgia, and have two children, Graham and Macy.

www.worship360group.com
email: info@worship360group.com
www.rivercrestmusic.com